AQA HISTORY

GCSE 9–1

Conflict and Tension between East and West 1945–1972

by Andrew Wallace and
Nathalie Harty

■SCHOLASTIC

Authors Andrew Wallace and Nathalie Harty

Series Editor Paul Martin

Reviewer Paul Martin

Editorial team Aidan Gill, Turnstone Solutions Limited, Rachel Morgan, Vicki Yates, Kirsty Taylor, Liz Evans

Typesetting Daniel Prescott, Couper Street Type Co

Cover design Dipa Mistry

App development Hannah Barnett, Phil Crothers and RAIOSOFT International Pvt Ltd

Photographs
cover and title page: United States of America against USSR boxing gloves, © Kevkhiev Yury/Dreamstime.com; pages 10 and 11: flags: USSR, Mikhail Mishchenko/Shutterstock; UK, Sunflowerr/Shutterstock; USA, Sunflowerr/Shutterstock; page 10: Joseph Stalin, US Army Signal Corps/Wikimedia Commons; Nikita S. Khrushchev, Bundesarchiv Bild/Wikimedia Commons; Leonid Brezhnev, Commons Bundesarchiv/Wikimedia Commons; Winston Churchill, BiblioArchives Library Archives/Wikimedia Commons; Clement Attlee, Wikimedia Commons; page 11: Franklin Delano Roosevelt, Wikimedia Commons; Harry Truman, National Archives and Records Administration, Office of Presidential Libraries, Harry S. Truman Library/Wikimedia Commons; Richard M. Nixon, Wikimedia Commons; Dwight Eisenhower, Wikimedia Commons; Lyndon Johnson, Wikimedia Commons; John F. Kennedy, National Archives and Records Administration/Wikimedia Commons; page 12: USA flag, Wikimedia Commons; USSR flag, Wikimedia Commons; page 13: Yalta summit, photograph from the Army Signal Corps Collection in the U.S. National Archives/Wikimedia Commons; page 15: Potsdam conference, U.S. Government/Wikimedia Commons; page 16: nuclear bomb aftermath, Wikimedia Commons; page 17: Winston Churchill, BiblioArchives Library Archives/Wikimedia Commons; 'Iron curtain' cartoon, Associated Newspapers Ltd./Solo Syndication; page 19: Harry Truman, National Archives and Records Administration, Office of Presidential Libraries, Harry S. Truman Library/Wikimedia Commons; walnut, Pixabay; Joseph Stalin, US Army Signal Corps/Wikimedia Commons; page 20: first deutsche mark, Wikimedia Commons; page 21: Berlin Airlift, Wikimedia Commons; page 23: Chinese postage stamp, Wikimedia Commons; page 28: 'Bert ducks and covers' cartoon, Wikimedia Commons; page 29: NATO symbol, ShadeDesign/Shutterstock; page 31: Saturn IB launch, Wikimedia Commons; page 32: Hungarian Uprising, FOTO-FORTEPAN-Nagy Gyula [CC BY-SA 3.0]/Wikimedia Commons; page 37: Berlin Wall, Wikimedia Commons; page 38: President Kennedy, Wikimedia Commons; page 38: cartoon showing Khrushchev looking over Berlin War, Don Wright/The Miami News/Solo Syndication; page 41: John F. Kennedy, National Archives and Records Administration/Wikimedia Commons; Fidel Castro, emkaplin/Shutterstock; Nikita S. Khrushchev, Bundesarchiv Bild/Wikimedia Commons; page 45: Brezhnev Russian doll, VisualPharm/SOFTICONS; page 47: Leonid Brezhnev, Commons Bundesarchiv/Wikimedia Commons; page 51: 'How to close the gap?' cartoon, Sarin Images/GRANGER; page 53: 'Why can't we work together in mutual trust' cartoon, Associated Newspapers Ltd./Solo Syndication; page 59: Chinese Propaganda Poster, Wikimedia Commons; page 74: cartoon on the Korean War by Low, © David Low/ Associated Newspaper/Solo Syndication; 'The rival buses' cartoon by E. H. Shepard from Punch, © Granger; page 75: Walt Disney and Wehrner von Braun, Wikimedia Commons

Illustration
QBS Learning

Designed using Adobe InDesign

Published in the UK by Scholastic Education, 2020
Book End, Range Road, Witney, Oxfordshire, OX29 0YD
A division of Scholastic Limited
London – New York – Toronto – Sydney – Auckland
Mexico City – New Delhi – Hong Kong
SCHOLASTIC and associated logos are trademarks and/or registered trademarks of Scholastic Inc.
www.scholastic.co.uk
© 2020 Scholastic Limited
1 2 3 4 5 6 7 8 9   0 1 2 3 4 5 6 7 8 9

British Library Cataloguing-in-Publication Data
A catalogue record for this book is available from the British Library.

ISBN 978-1407-18338-1

Printed and bound by Bell and Bain Ltd, Glasgow
Papers used by Scholastic Limited are made from wood grown in sustainable forests.

Acknowledgements
The publishers gratefully acknowledge permission to reproduce the following copyright material: **Mirrorpix** for 'Back to where it all started (Z Bomb)' and 'Of course, Mr. Dubček' cartoons by Michael Cummings, (*Daily Express*, 1953 and 1968); **Taylor & Francis Group** for extract from *Common Sense and Nuclear Warfare* by Bertrand Russell, (© Routledge Classics, an imprint of Taylor and Francis (Books) Limited UK, 2010)

Every effort has been made to trace copyright holders for the works reproduced in this book, and the publishers apologise for any inadvertent omissions.

Note from the publisher:
Please use this product in conjunction with the official specification and sample assessment materials. Ask your teacher if you are unsure where to find them.

Contents

Check your answers on the free revision app or at www.scholastic.co.uk/gcse

Features of this guide

The best way to retain information is to take an active approach to revision.

Throughout this book, you will find lots of features that will make your revision an active, successful process.

SNAPIT!

Use the Snap it! feature in the revision app to take pictures of key concepts and information. Great for revision on the go!

Regular exercise helps stimulate the brain and will help you relax.

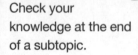

DOIT!

Activities to embed your knowledge and understanding and prepare you for the exams.

Find methods of relaxation that work for you throughout the revision period.

NAILIT!

Words shown in **purple bold** can be found in the glossary on page 79.

Succinct and vital tips on how to do well in your exam.

STRETCHIT!

Provides content that stretches you further.

CHECKIT!

Check your knowledge at the end of a subtopic.

Revise in pairs or small groups and deliver presentations on topics to each other.

PRACTICE PAPERS

Full mock-exam papers to practise before you sit the real thing!

FOR HIGH-MARK QUESTIONS, SPEND TIME **PLANNING** YOUR ANSWER!

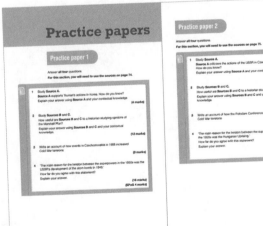

FREE REVISION APP

- The **free revision app** can be downloaded to your mobile phone (iOS and Android), making **on the go revision** easy.

- Use the revision calendar to help map out your revision in the lead-up to the exam.

- Complete multiple-choice questions and create your own SNAP**IT!** revision cards.

www.scholastic.co.uk/gcse

Online answers and additional resources

All of the tasks in this book are designed to get you thinking and to consolidate your understanding through thought and application. Therefore, it is important to write your own answers before checking. Some questions include answer lines where you need to fill in your answer in the book. Other questions require you to use a separate piece of paper so that you can draft your response and work out the best way of answering.

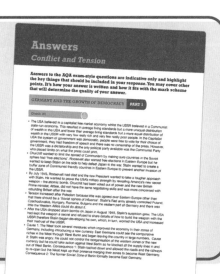

Get plenty of sleep, especially the night before an exam.

LOOK AFTER YOURSELF

Help your brain by looking after your whole body!

Once you have worked through a section, you can check your answers to Do it!, Stretch it!, Check it! and the exam practice papers on the app or at **www.scholastic.co.uk/gcse**.

Topic focus:
Wider world depth study

Conflict and Tension between East and West, 1945-1972

This is a *Wider World Depth Study*. You will have studied the **causes and events of the Cold War** and **why it proved difficult to resolve the tensions** which arose during the Cold War. You will also have considered **the role of key individuals and groups** in shaping change and how they were affected by and influenced international relations.

This topic appears in Section B (the second half) of the first AQA exam (Paper 1) and is worth 25% of your final GCSE mark.

Paper 1: Understanding the Modern World Time: 2 hours	Paper 2: Shaping the Nation Time: 2 hours
Section A: Period Study	Section A: Thematic Study
Section B: Wider World Depth Study	Section B: British Depth Study

In Paper 1, Section B you will face four questions which test three different skills:

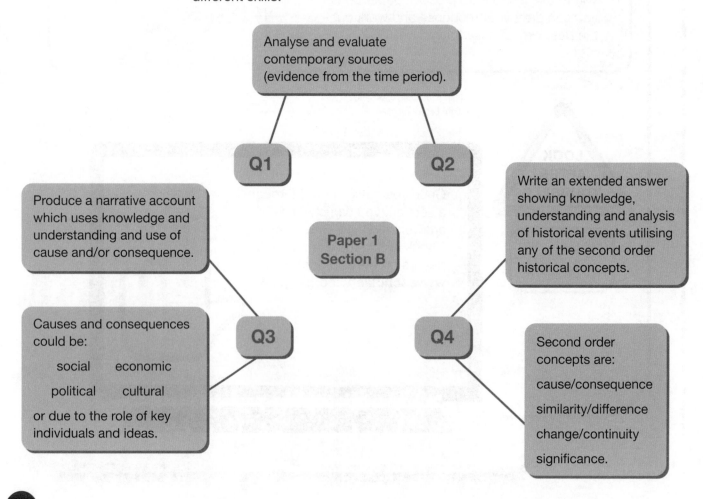

Analyse and evaluate contemporary sources (evidence from the time period).

Q1

Q2

Write an extended answer showing knowledge, understanding and analysis of historical events utilising any of the second order historical concepts.

Produce a narrative account which uses knowledge and understanding and use of cause and/or consequence.

Paper 1 Section B

Causes and consequences could be:

social   economic

political   cultural

or due to the role of key individuals and ideas.

Q3

Q4

Second order concepts are:

cause/consequence

similarity/difference

change/continuity

significance.

The first and second questions require **the analysis and evaluation of sources**. One source is supplied for the first question and two sources for the second. Different types of sources will be used, including visual and written sources.

The third question requires a **narrative account**, which uses **knowledge, understanding and analysis of cause and/or consequence.**

The fourth question requires **knowledge, understanding and analysis of historical events** utilising any of the second order historical concepts:

* cause/consequence
* similarity/difference
* change/continuity
* significance.

This will be an essay question requiring a judgement. It is an extended response which will give you the opportunity to demonstrate your ability to construct and develop a sustained line of reasoning which is coherent, relevant, substantiated and logically structured.

Contemporary Source evaluation

These might include:

* political cartoons
* speeches
* letters
* diary entries
* newspaper reports.

When analysing and evaluating contemporary sources you will need to focus on:

* Provenance – comment on: who created the source? What type of source is it? When, where and why was the source produced?

* Content – you should describe and refer to points being made in the source

* Contextual knowledge – you need to show the examiner what extra knowledge you have which helps you make a decision about the message of the source and, for question 2, how useful you think the source is for telling us about the topic.

Keep a close watch on the time in the exam. Don't spend more than one hour on the section you complete first or you will not have enough time to complete the other section properly.

Take special care over spelling, punctuation and grammar as there are four extra marks available for these.

Timeline

Conflict and tension between East and West, 1945–72

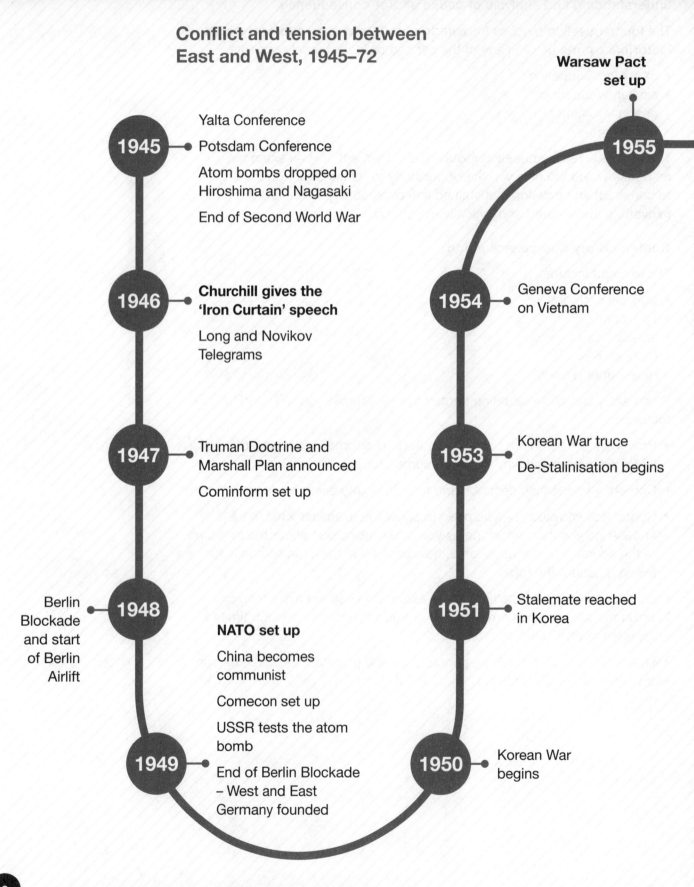

1945
- Yalta Conference
- Potsdam Conference
- Atom bombs dropped on Hiroshima and Nagasaki
- End of Second World War

1946
- **Churchill gives the 'Iron Curtain' speech**
- Long and Novikov Telegrams

1947
- Truman Doctrine and Marshall Plan announced
- Cominform set up

1948
- Berlin Blockade and start of Berlin Airlift

1949
- **NATO set up**
- China becomes communist
- Comecon set up
- USSR tests the atom bomb
- End of Berlin Blockade – West and East Germany founded

1950
- Korean War begins

1951
- Stalemate reached in Korea

1953
- Korean War truce
- De-Stalinisation begins

1954
- Geneva Conference on Vietnam

1955
- **Warsaw Pact set up**

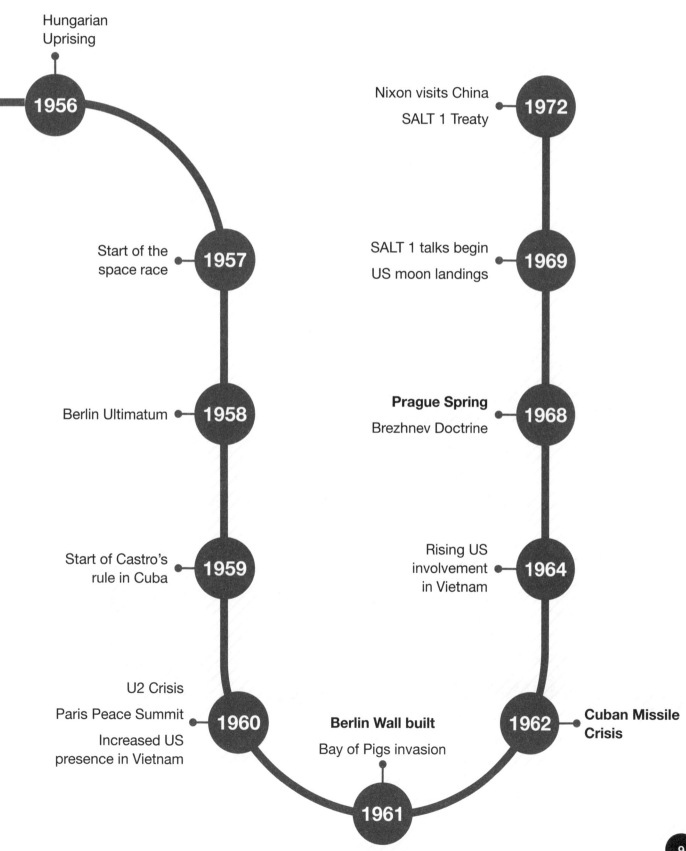

Hungarian
Uprising

1956

Nixon visits China
SALT 1 Treaty

1972

Start of the
space race

1957

SALT 1 talks begin
US moon landings

1969

Berlin Ultimatum

1958

Prague Spring
Brezhnev Doctrine

1968

Start of Castro's
rule in Cuba

1959

Rising US
involvement
in Vietnam

1964

U2 Crisis

Paris Peace Summit

Increased US
presence in Vietnam

1960

Berlin Wall built

Bay of Pigs invasion

**Cuban Missile
Crisis**

1962

1961

9

USSR

Joseph Stalin

Stalin controlled communist USSR from 1928 until his death in 1953. Responsible for the USSR's approach at Yalta and Potsdam. Keen to protect the Soviet 'sphere'.

Nikita Khrushchev

In control of communist USSR from 1953 until he was removed in 1964. In charge during the Hungarian Uprising, construction of the Berlin Wall and the Cuban Missile Crisis. Also in charge during the period of the 'Thaw' in relations.

Leonid Brezhnev

In control of communist USSR from 1964 until his death in 1982. Involved in Prague Spring and SALT 1. A hardliner, forced to seek reduction in nuclear weapons.

Key allied communist leaders

Mao Tse-tung Leader of China 1949–76

Fidel Castro Leader of Cuba 1959–2008

Kim Il-Sung Leader of North Korea 1948–94

Ho Chi Minh President of North Vietnam 1954–69

UK

Winston Churchill

Prime Minister of the democratic UK, 1940–45 and 1951–55. Led during the Second World War and Yalta Conference. Gave the famous 'Iron Curtain' speech. Forced to recognise UK's secondary role between two superpowers.

Clement Attlee

Prime Minister of democratic UK 1945–51. Involved in Potsdam and Berlin Airlift. More interested in the welfare state than in international relations.

USA

Franklin D. Roosevelt

President of the democratic USA from 1933 until his death in 1945. Led during the Second World War and Yalta Conference. His death gave the more experienced Stalin an advantage in negotiations over the new leaders Attlee and Truman.

Harry S. Truman

President of the democratic USA from 1945 until voted out in 1952. Led during the dropping of the atom bombs on Japan and the Korean War. His Truman Doctrine took a tough line on communist expansion.

Richard Nixon

President of the democratic USA from 1968 until his resignation in 1974. Oversaw the moon landings, 'Ping-Pong diplomacy' with China, SALT 1.

Dwight D. Eisenhower

President of the democratic USA from 1952 until voted out in 1960. Responsible for US approaches to Korean War, arms race and space race. A war hero who wanted to deal with the Soviets firmly.

Lyndon B. Johnson

President of the democratic USA from 1963 until he stood down in 1968. Led during the Prague Spring and was responsible for increasing involvement of USA in Vietnam.

John F. Kennedy

President of the democratic USA from 1960 until his assassination in 1963. Involved in the Bay of Pigs invasion, Berlin Wall and Cuban Missile Crisis.

Part One:
The origins of the Cold War

The end of the Second World War

During the Second World War, although fighting on the same side, the Western allies did not forget the Nazi–Soviet Pact of 1939 and remained suspicious that Stalin might arrange a separate peace deal with Hitler. At the end of the Second World War, with their common enemies defeated, the differences in the opinions of the wartime allies became clear.

Contrasting ideologies of the USA and the USSR

West	East
Democratic	Dictatorship
Capitalist	Communist
Free market economy	Government-run economy
Average living standards	Lower than average living standards
Freedom of speech	Limits on free speech
Uneven distribution of wealth – more poor people	More equal distribution of wealth – fewer people were very rich or very poor

The Yalta Conference, February 1945

By early 1945, the Allies were making strong gains in the war and victory was almost certain. The leaders of the three main Allied powers – Churchill, Roosevelt and Stalin – met at Yalta to decide on what would happen once the war was over. Despite their different aims, several important decisions were made.

Churchill: I am not convinced that Stalin can be trusted. I am suspicious of the spread of communist ideas in the countries the USSR now control; there must be democratic elections held in these places after the war.

Roosevelt: Countries everywhere should have free elections. I have no intention of helping Britain maintain their Empire. I will give Stalin the benefit of the doubt and hope he helps to defeat Japan and joins the United Nations.

Stalin: I have no intention of allowing the USSR to be attacked again. I will create a 'buffer zone' of friendly communist states. There will be 'free' elections.

The aims of Stalin, Churchill and Roosevelt at the Yalta Conference, February 1945.

Elections to be held in liberated countries

United Nations set up

Reparations to be paid by Germany

Occupation of Germany by victorious nations (Britain, France, USA and USSR)

Punishment of war criminals

Eastern Europe to be under Soviet 'sphere of influence'

Stalin agreed to help defeat Japan

Decisions made at Yalta about Europe's future.

DO IT!

Take a sheet of paper and cover up the definitions following each letter in the EUROPES acrostic. Write down what each letter stands for. Uncover the definitions and check if you were right!

The Potsdam Conference, July 1945

In July, leaders of the three main Allied powers met again at Potsdam. However, there had been some changes in the international situation since the Yalta Conference.

Aims of Truman and Attlee

26 July 1945 Churchill loses election, Attlee new UK Prime Minister!

2 May 1945 Hitler dead! The war will soon be over!

13 April 1945 Roosevelt dead! Truman now President of the USA

16 July 1945 12 million people in the USA see A-bomb test!

Key changes since Yalta

Stalin's aims remained the same as at Yalta, but the aims of the other leaders had changed. The new American President, Harry Truman, wanted to:

- take a tougher approach than Roosevelt in dealing with the USSR; he famously said he was 'tired of babying the Soviets'

- prove the USA's military strength by revealing their secret weapon, the atom bomb.

The new British Prime Minister, Clement Attlee, did not have the same negotiating skills as Churchill and was more concerned with getting on with governing Britain. Therefore the British Foreign Secretary, Ernest Bevin, discussed Britain's priorities with Stalin. These were to:

- maintain influence over countries in the British Empire, like Egypt and India

- improve relations between Britain and the USSR by establishing trade links

- receive some of the **reparations** money to be paid by Germany.

Besides these differences, now that their common enemy was defeated, there was less reason for the Allies to work together. Also, now that Truman had the atom bomb, the most powerful weapon in the world, the USA no longer needed Soviet help to defeat Japan.

DO IT!

Create and complete your own copy of the following table, to show the aims of the Big Three at the Yalta and Potsdam conferences.

Country	Name of leader and their main aims at Yalta	Name of leader and their main aims at Potsdam
UK		
USA		
USSR		

Disagreements at Potsdam

There were two major areas on which the leaders disagreed at Potsdam:

1 How to deal with Germany

2 Soviet control in Eastern Europe

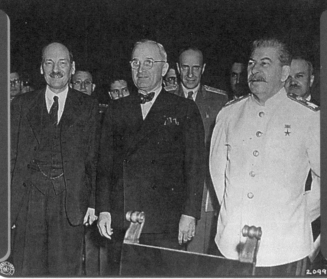

Western view: Stalin should allow free elections in Eastern Europe; it should not become a Soviet Empire.

Western view: It would be a mistake to punish Germany harshly. We want a strong Germany as a trading partner. We do not want to make Germany seek revenge and start another war.

Stalin's view: I demand $10 billion in reparations from Germany to help us recover from the war. 20 million Soviet citizens died and the country has been devastated. Also, I want to make Germany weak to protect the USSR from future threats.

Stalin's view: Soviet control of Eastern Europe will create a 'buffer zone' to guard against future attacks.

Clement Attlee (left), Harry Truman (centre) and Josef Stalin (right)

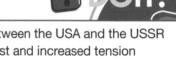

Study the table below. Then write a paragraph to explain why tensions between the USA and the USSR increased after Potsdam. Make sure you use the phrase 'this led to mistrust and increased tension because …'

What was agreed at Potsdam …	What was not agreed at Potsdam …
Germany was to be split into four zones, each run by an allied army.	There was little agreement over Eastern Europe. Stalin's **Red Army** already controlled Poland, Czechoslovakia, Hungary, Romania, Bulgaria and the eastern part of Germany, and there was little the Western Allies could do about it.
Germany would be de-militarised.	
The Nazi Party would be banned and war criminals put on trial.	Stalin was not given a naval base in the Mediterranean. He saw this as evidence that the Western allies mistrusted him.
Reparations – each of the Allies could 'take what they wanted' from their own zone of Germany.	

NAILIT!

Make sure you understand why there were more disagreements at the Potsdam Conference than at Yalta, and what these disagreements were about.

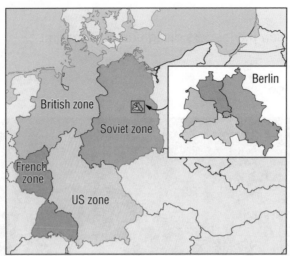

The division of Germany and Berlin after the Second World War.

The division of Germany

As agreed at Potsdam, Germany was divided into four zones, controlled by the USA, Britain, France and the USSR. The capital of Germany, Berlin, was also divided into four zones. It was situated deep inside the Soviet zone, so much depended on the goodwill of the USSR to allow supplies into the western zones of Berlin.

The effect that dropping the atom bomb had on post-war superpower relations

On 6 August 1945, in order to bring the war in Asia to an end, the USA dropped an atom bomb on the Japanese city of Hiroshima. The city was destroyed and 80,000 people were killed in an instant. Tens of thousands were wounded and suffered from the effects of radiation. Three days later, another atom bomb was dropped on the Japanese city of Nagasaki, causing similar devastation. Japan did surrender and the war ended on 15 August 1945. However, there was evidence that Japan may have surrendered anyway and that this event was an attempt by the USA to show off its military strength and frighten the **Soviet Union**.

This event increased tension and mistrust between East and West.

- As a result of the work of Soviet spies, Stalin already knew that the Americans were developing the atom bomb when Truman told him at Potsdam. He was furious that the USA had been keeping secrets from him.

- Truman told Stalin very little about the atom bomb at Potsdam and later made it clear that he would not share the new technology with the USSR.

- The huge destruction caused by the bombs proved that the Americans now had the most powerful weapon in the world. This gave Stalin even more reason to fear the USA.

- It had been agreed at Yalta that the USSR would help defeat Japan, but it looked as though Truman had gone back on this by dropping the bombs to end the war. However, ending the war without Soviet help meant that the USA did not fear a situation developing as it had in Eastern Europe, as no Soviet troops were present.

- To try and compete with the USA, the USSR began developing its own atom bomb. This was tested in 1949. The arms race had begun.

DO IT!

Take a photo of this map and write a paragraph to explain the potential problems of the geographical location of Berlin.

The devastation caused by the atom bomb dropped on Hiroshima on 6 August 1945.

The Iron Curtain and the evolution of East–West rivalry

Soviet expansion in Eastern Europe

Churchill was concerned for the countries under Soviet control on the eastern side of what he called the 'Iron Curtain'. Although in 1946 it was only a line on a map, 'the Iron Curtain' would later become a physical barrier, with armed guards and barbed wire separating east from west.

From Stettin in the Baltic to Trieste in the Adriatic, an Iron Curtain has descended across the continent [Europe].

Speech given by Winston Churchill during a visit to the USA in March 1946.

DO IT!

1 Write three or four bullet points to describe what is happening in this cartoon.

2 Do you think the cartoonist supports the USSR? How can you tell?

When Churchill made his 'Iron Curtain' speech, only some of Eastern Europe had become communist. However, by 1949 all of Eastern Europe was under communist rule and most of these countries were under the influence of the USSR. Despite communist governments being 'elected' to power, many of the elections were fixed so that the Communists would definitely win. Opponents were often intimidated and in some cases killed. These countries became **satellite states** of the USSR.

This cartoon was published in a British newspaper in May 1946. It shows the British Foreign Secretary, Ernest Bevin, and the American Secretary of State, James Byrnes, on the left, and the Soviet Foreign Minister, Vyacheslav Molotov, at the top.

Following the end of the war in May 1945, the **eastern part of Germany** was under the control of the Soviet Army. From 1948, the Soviet forces began transferring authority to German communist leaders. By October 1949, **East Germany** had become a full satellite state of the USSR.

In **Poland**, 'rigged' elections in January 1947 put the Communists firmly in charge. Opposition parties had been threatened and the election results were adjusted.

Soviet expansion in Eastern Europe by 1949

USSR

The gradual takeover of **Hungary** by Communists was completed on 18 August 1949, when Hungary became the People's Republic of Hungary. Opposition politicians had been imprisoned and Church leaders attacked.

A left-wing coalition won the 1945 election in **Czechoslovakia**. In 1946 the Communists were the largest party within the coalition. In February 1948, they banned other parties and made the country a communist 'one-party state'.

BERLIN

EAST GERMANY

POLAND

WEST GERMANY

CZECHOSLOVAKIA

AUSTRIA

HUNGARY

ITALY

YUGOSLAVIA

ROMANIA

BULGARIA

ALBANIA

Romania was occupied by Soviet troops in 1944 and became a satellite of the USSR in September 1947.

In **Yugoslavia,** Communist Party leader, Marshal Tito, was elected President in November 1945. He was an ally of Stalin at first, but wanted Yugoslavia to be independent from the USSR. Tensions arose between the two Communist leaders, causing a split between them.

Communists gained control of **Albania** immediately after the war, with little opposition. A new people's assembly was elected in December 1945, which voted to abolish the monarchy and formally declare Albania a communist state.

Bulgaria was officially declared a communist state in September 1946, after the people voted to abolish the monarchy and the Communists executed the leaders of other political parties.

DO IT!

1 Take a photo of this map and then write a paragraph that explains whether or not you think the concerns of the USA about the spread of communism were justified.

2 Using the information in the boxes, create a timeline of the communist takeover of Eastern Europe.

US policies: the Truman Doctrine and Marshall Plan

By February 1947, Britain could no longer afford to continue providing aid to the Greek government in their civil war against the communists. Without British support, a communist victory became far more likely. President Truman decided that this must not be allowed to happen.

On 12 March 1947, Truman made a speech to **Congress**, calling for the US government to provide financial and military aid to any foreign country threatened by communism. The ideas in his speech became known as the Truman **Doctrine**.

The US government gave Greece, and Greece's neighbour Turkey, a total of 400 million dollars in aid. With this help, the Communists in the Greek civil war were defeated.

In June 1947, **US Secretary of State**, George Marshall, announced 17 billion dollars of aid for European countries over the next four years. This 'Marshall Plan' money was to be used to repair war damage and to build up industry. The idea was that people would be less likely to support communism if they had jobs, homes and food.

> It must be the policy of the United States to support free people who are resisting attempted subjugation by armed minorities or outside pressure.

Speech given by President Truman in March 1947. This policy became known as the Truman Doctrine.

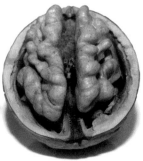

President Truman described the Truman Doctrine and Marshall Plan as *'Two halves of the same walnut'*. This means two plans that had the same aim – **containment** of communism.

Stalin's reaction to US policies

Stalin was furious and felt threatened by the Truman Doctrine and Marshall Plan. He saw it as the USA using money to take control of European countries. Soviet satellite states were forbidden from accepting Marshall Aid. The Soviet government also set up the following to support the satellite states.

- Cominform (Communist Information Bureau) helped European Communist parties work more closely together and follow Soviet directions

- Comecon (Council for Mutual Economic Assistance) encouraged trade between Communist states. It massively favoured the USSR as a market for the goods of satellite states.

> This is nothing more than dollar imperialism! Part of the American plan for world domination! Why should our enemy, Germany, receive any money after the damage and destruction they caused in the war?

Stalin's reaction to the Marshall Plan.

Yugoslavia

The Communist the leader of Yugoslavia, Marshal Tito, had refused to be controlled by the Soviet Union. In 1948, Tito's relations with Stalin finally broke down; Russian troops were sent to Yugoslavia's borders and trade between the countries ended. Tito and Yugoslavia only survived with the help of Marshall Aid.

The Berlin Blockade and Airlift, 1948–49

After the destruction of the Second World War, Germany was in economic chaos.

The Western Allies wanted:

- Germany to rebuild its industries so the German people had jobs, homes and food, and would become a strong trading partner

- to avoid another war by making Germany economically stable.

Stalin wanted:

- to keep Germany weak as punishment for war damage and to prevent another invasion of the USSR

- to drive the Western Allies out of West Berlin, so that the whole city would be under Soviet control.

The West took several measures which improved the economy in their zones of Germany. Stalin was unhappy that his wartime enemy was being strengthened; he believed this was a deliberate move against him. At the same time, there was considerable poverty and unemployment in East Germany. East Germans could see the comparative riches in the West through West Berlin and began leaving the country in large numbers. Then, in June 1948, Britain and France introduced a new currency in their zones – the Deutsche Mark – to improve trade with the West.

Events that led to the Berlin Blockade.

In January 1947, the British and Americans combined their zones into one – Bi-zonia (the French added their zone in August 1948 to become Tri-zonia)

In early 1948, Marshall Aid flooded into Western Germany and West Berlin

=

Western Germany started to recover, but Eastern Germany was still in poverty

+

In June 1948, Britain and France introduced the Deutsche Mark in their zone, which furthered economy recovery

=

In June 1948, Stalin blockaded West Berlin

Stalin was angry. He could not control the reorganisation of the Western zones or the new currency, but he could take action against West Berlin, as it was located deep in the Soviet zone (see map on page 16). On 24 June 1948, Stalin blocked all the supply lines in and out of West Berlin. Roads, railways and canals were all closed, cutting off 2 million people living in West Berlin. He hoped that by doing this, West Berlin would become reliant on Soviet help and he could force the Western Allies out of the city altogether.

The Berlin Blockade and Airlift in numbers

- Stalin blockaded supply routes in and out of West Berlin for 318 days (11 months).
- American and British planes prepared to drop supplies into West Berlin. The first took off on 26 June 1948.
- 275,000 flights in total carried 1.5 million tons of supplies.
- A plane landed every 3 minutes.
- On one day flights brought in 13,000 tons of supplies. Berlin only needed 6000 tons a day to survive.
- The airlift continued until 30 September 1949, in order to build up a reserve of supplies.

Stalin eventually backed down and allowed railways and roads to re-open. The West kept its presence deep in communist territory, which meant Berlin would continue to be a **pressure point** of the Cold War.

Consequences of the Berlin Blockade and Airlift

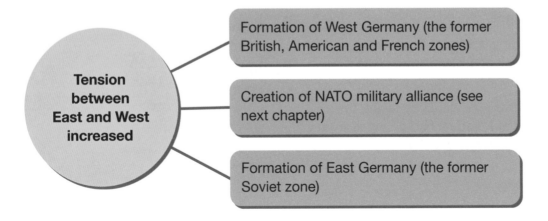

Tension between East and West increased

- Formation of West Germany (the former British, American and French zones)
- Creation of NATO military alliance (see next chapter)
- Formation of East Germany (the former Soviet zone)

DOIT!

Complete this table.

Who was most responsible for increasing tension and causing the Cold War?	USA?	USSR?	Both/ neither?
Soviet sphere of influence in Europe			
The 'free elections' were rigged			
Stalin's wish for a buffer zone			
The Marshall Plan			
The atom bomb			
Fear of communism			
Soviet troops in Eastern Europe			

NAILIT!

There is no right or wrong answer to the question who was most responsible for causing the Cold War, you have to decide what your own personal opinion is. In the exam, make sure that you explain how both sides contributed to the tension rising before reaching your final judgement. Be balanced but decisive.

CHECKIT! ✓

1. Explain two ways in which the USA and USSR had contrasting attitudes and **ideologies**.

2. Describe the aims of Churchill, Roosevelt and Stalin at the Yalta Conference.

3. Explain why the situation facing the leaders at Potsdam had changed from the one facing them at Yalta.

4. Suggest why tension between East and West increased after Potsdam.

5. Explain why the dropping of the atom bomb further increased mistrust.

6. Explain two causes and two consequences of the Berlin Blockade.

Part Two:
The development of the Cold War

The significance of events in Asia for superpower relations

China

1949 was a key year: Mao Tse-tung declared a Communist People's Republic in China. This meant the Communists, with the support of the USSR, had won the Chinese Civil War, which had raged since 1927. The Americans had supported the defeated Nationalists under Chiang Kai-shek. The Nationalists fled to Taiwan, where they continued to be recognised as the government of China by the West.

Chinese postage stamp commemorating the Treaty of Friendship, February 1950: Stalin (left) and Mao (right) shake hands.

Significance for superpower relations

1 The USSR had helped a massive nation become communist and seemed to have gained a very important ally. This support continued in 1950 with the Treaty of Friendship.

2 Western containment had failed and there was now another huge communist state for the USA to be worried about, as China had a seat on the UN Security Council. The US government secretly issued NSC-68, which funded planning and development for a possible war against communist states if containment failed to stop the communist advance around the world. It involved a massive build-up of atomic weapons and ground forces.

3 The USA and other Western countries claimed Chiang should represent China at the UN, but the USSR insisted on Mao. The USSR boycotted the UN Security Council in protest. This created a deadlock at the UN which would have an impact on other areas of the world, especially Korea (see page 24).

4 Many ordinary people in the West, and particularly in the USA, were very concerned as a huge country had seemingly 'joined' the opposing side. Fear was also heightened because in the same year, the USSR had developed its own atom bomb.

> ### Details of the Treaty of Friendship:
>
> - $300m aid to China from USSR, to be spent on Soviet materials
> - 95 per cent to be repaid at high interest
> - 8000 students allowed to study Science, Technology and Maths in the USSR
> - 20,000 Soviet 'experts' deployed at China's cost
> - Mining rights and port facilities given to the USSR

DO IT!

Photograph the detail of the Treaty of Friendship. Create cartoon frames to sum it up in images and numbers. Who benefitted?

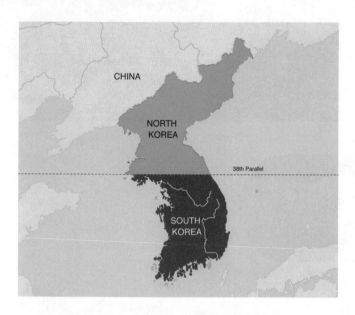

Korea

Korea had been part of the Japanese Empire since 1910. When Japan was defeated in 1945, it was agreed at the Potsdam Conference that, like Germany, Korea would be divided. It was occupied by Soviet troops in the North and US troops in the South. In May 1948 the North officially became a communist state, under Soviet-trained Kim Il-Sung. The South was capitalist, under Syngman Rhee, supported by the USA.

The division of Korea in 1945. North of the 38th Parallel was occupied by the USSR (red). South of the 38th Parallel was occupied by the USA (green).

The build up to and events of the Korean War

1949	Kim wanted Stalin to support a full invasion of the South. This would bring Soviet troops into contact with 7500 US troops, and could ignite a 'hot' war.
February 1950	Stalin provided weapons and tactical knowledge to North Korea. The Chinese gave support across their border with North Korea for an invasion of the South.
June 1950	North Korea invaded the South. The UN appealed for a ceasefire. When that was ignored, the UN agreed to send troops to drive the Northern troops back. The USSR could not veto this, because they were boycotting the UN over China.
September 1950	UN forces from 16 countries under US command, led by General Douglas MacArthur, landed at Inchon, in South Korea, and pushed the North Koreans back to the original border, the 38th Parallel.
October 1950	Mao sent in Chinese troops to support the North. The UN forces were pushed back southwards. The communists captured the South's capital, Seoul.
April 1951	MacArthur was sacked by President Truman. He had overstepped the mark in calling for the use of nuclear weapons.
June 1951	UN forces drove the communist forces back northwards. By June, they had reached a stalemate. Tentative peace negotiations began.
July 1953	A ceasefire was agreed – not a peace settlement. The borders were back virtually at the 38th Parallel.

Significance for superpower relations

1 The Korean War raised the profile of Mao's Chinese Red Army, and the possible threat it posed to capitalist countries in Asia. For the West, this added to the threat of communism, which now had the support of another powerful army.

2 US President Eisenhower presented the **Domino Theory**, which became very popular in the USA. If Communists could invade a capitalist country like South Korea, where would the spread of communism end? This theory would have a big impact on later decisions the USA made about intervening in foreign conflicts, particularly with regard to Vietnam.

DO IT!

Create a Post-it™ timeline of 1950–53 with dates on one set and events on another set. Match the dates to the events.

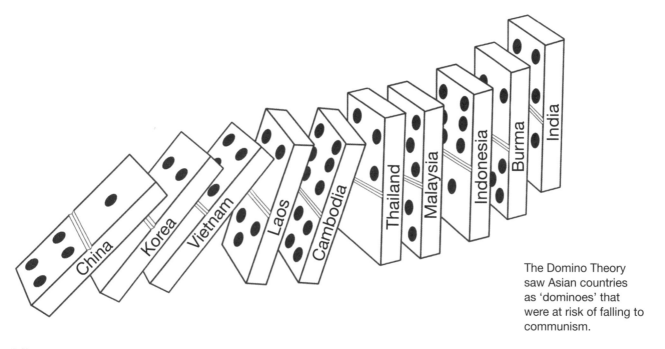

The Domino Theory saw Asian countries as 'dominoes' that were at risk of falling to communism.

Vietnam

Before the Second World War, Vietnam, Laos and Cambodia were part of the French Empire. When France was defeated, the Japanese took control. Ho Chi Minh led Nationalists and Communists in fighting against the Japanese. When the war ended in 1945, Ho felt sure his supporters would gain some freedom, and proclaimed the Democratic Republic of Vietnam.

However, the French returned to re-establish their control. Ho's fighters turned their anger on the French, and fought them until 1954, using **guerrilla warfare**. The **Viet Minh** astonished the West by demolishing the French at Dien Bien Phu. The French had to leave Vietnam, and Eisenhower felt sure that the Domino Theory was being played out. He felt compelled to act.

1954–63

Eisenhower called the 1954 Geneva Conference, which divided Vietnam. The North was communist, under Ho Chi Minh, and the South was capitalist, under President Diem. Elections to reunite the country and decide who should rule it were scheduled for July 1956. However, Eisenhower did not allow these elections to take place – he was worried the Communists would win.

The division of Vietnam from 1954, as decided at the Geneva Conference.

DOIT!

Write down the numbers '17' and '38' and the letters 'K' and 'V'. Draw horizontal lines through the centre of each. You'll see 38 and K are symmetrical, 17 and V are not. That may help remind you that 38 (parallel) refers to Korea, 'K', and 17 (parallel) refers to Vietnam, 'V'.

New Look policy

The USA sent to South Vietnam more:
- money
- equipment
- political experts
- military experts.

The 'Domino Theory' led to Eisenhower's 'New Look' policy from 1953. This was different from the policy of containment, in that it put more faith (and money) in the air force's ability to avoid having to put troops on the ground. The USA was committing to keeping South Vietnam from falling to communism, but without using US soldiers to fight a guerrilla war.

All the while, the Viet Minh were consistently striking military and civilian targets in South Vietnam.

Changes, 1960–63

1 The National Liberation Front (NLF, or **Vietcong** as they became known) developed the Ho Chi Minh Trail to support Vietcong fighters in Diem's South Vietnam.

2 In the USA, Kennedy became President. He raised the numbers of US military and political 'experts' in Vietnam to 16,000 by 1963.

3 In 1963, both Diem and Kennedy were assassinated. The new US President, Lyndon Johnson, raised US military involvement dramatically (see page 48).

The USA was getting increasingly involved in Vietnam. It was about to become involved in a war from 1964–75 that was unpopular with the American public, and which the USA could neither win, nor afford to lose.

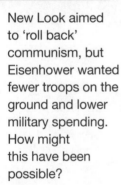

STRETCHIT!

New Look aimed to 'roll back' communism, but Eisenhower wanted fewer troops on the ground and lower military spending. How might this have been possible?

NAILIT!

The Vietcong (NLF) had the support of many civilians, as they were Vietnamese. They also did not need to fight traditionally. For example, their fighters did not wear military uniform, so they were difficult to pick out. The American 'experts' were easily spotted, especially in the capital, Saigon. Because of this, American casualties in 1963 were over 120.

Military rivalries

	USA	USSR
1949	13.5	13.4
1950	14.5	15.5
1951	33.3	20.1
1952	47.8	21.9
1953	49.6	25.5

Spending on arms in billions of US dollars.

The arms race

In 1945, atom bombs exploded at Hiroshima and Nagasaki, sending shock waves around the world. From this point, the superpowers began to try to out-do each other in new technological developments. Each side wanted to ensure they had more, and better, weapons than the opposition. Both sides accelerated as hard as they could. In this way, the arms race began.

DO IT!

Use the data above to create a graph.

USA

1945 USA detonates two atom bombs ('A-Bombs') over Japan to end the Second World War.

The USA was shocked at the pace of Soviet development. President Truman ordered a huge increase in US military spending.

1952 The USA successfully tests a hydrogen bomb ('H-Bomb').

USSR

The USSR was shocked and wanted to get equality in nuclear capability as quickly as possible. Pay for nuclear scientists was trebled, and more scientists were trained.

The USSR successfully tests its own A-Bomb. **1949**

The USSR successfully tests an 'H-Bomb'. **1953**

Both sides now accelerate spending on making nuclear weapons. Each side believes it is behind in the arms race.

1954 The USA detonates the largest device ever – equal to 15 million tons of TNT high explosive. The bombers to deliver these weapons (B-52s, which could fly 6000 miles) are being developed too.

The USSR detonates the largest device ever – equal to 50 million tons of TNT. **1961**

Actions and reactions of the arms race.

NAIL IT!

Before you revise this section, try to recall why the developments took place as they did. Jot them down. Check and re-evaluate your ideas after revision.

By 1962 therefore, both sides:

- had enough nuclear weapons to destroy the entire world

- had developed missile capability to carry these weapons across land, sea and air, including **ICBM**

- had used their nuclear muscle to push the other side hard, in an attempt to gain the upper hand in the Cold War. This policy was called **brinkmanship**.

The amount and power of weapons and missiles led to what became known as Mutually Assured Destruction (MAD). The frightening idea behind MAD is that neither side dare start a nuclear war because they will both be completely destroyed by it.

The significance of the arms race for the development of the Cold War

1 Fear hugely increased on both sides. Normal people were terrified of the possibility of nuclear war and were trained on what to do if there was a nuclear attack (see the poster and Stretch it! feature below).

2 The arms race made the tense situations that arose, such as the Berlin Blockade and Airlift in 1948 and Korea in 1951, even more tense because of the potential use of nuclear weapons. As leaders wanted to 'prove' their strength, it seemed increasingly possible they would use them. The potential for nuclear war became a very real possibility in 1962 over Cuba (see pages 39-42).

3 Europe had become more of a bystander in world affairs, and Europeans felt increasingly helpless. Churchill described the situation as a 'balance of terror'. Peace protests and 'ban the bomb' marches put pressure on European governments to try and limit the actions of the superpowers.

A US government public information poster about protection during nuclear attack, issued from 1951 onwards. There were animations, too, which also used 'Bert the Turtle'.

STRETCH IT!

Take a look at the original 'Duck and Cover' animation on YouTube. Does it help explain the fear in Western societies? What was Britain's attitude at this time? Search for CND and 'Protect and Survive' to find out more.

NATO

The North Atlantic Treaty Organisation (NATO) is a defensive military alliance, formed in 1949. It follows the European defence treaty signed in 1948 – the Treaty of Brussels.

For Western European countries, NATO brought the much needed might of the USA to join them in any attack against the USSR. For the USA, it meant having a foothold in Europe, as NATO allowed the US military access to Western European sites to station troops, weapons and air bases.

Belgium
UK
Canada
USA
Denmark
Portugal
France
Norway
Iceland
Netherlands
Luxembourg
Italy

The 12 original members of NATO.

NATO members agreed to act together against any country that attacked another member. It also meant the USA's front line for containment of the USSR's aggression was Western Europe.

Stalin called NATO an 'aggressive alliance', but did nothing immediately to retaliate. His focus at this time was on ending the Berlin Blockade without losing face.

Warsaw Pact

In 1955 West Germany was allowed to re-arm, and to join NATO. Khrushchev, who had replaced Stalin in 1953, had to react to the possibility of a powerfully armed West Germany on the borders of the Soviet sphere. Khrushchev had fought in the Second World War, and feared an armed Germany as part of NATO. As a response, he formed the Warsaw Pact of eight communist nations from behind the Iron Curtain. Their military response to an attack on any one of them would be the same as that of NATO – to support each other.

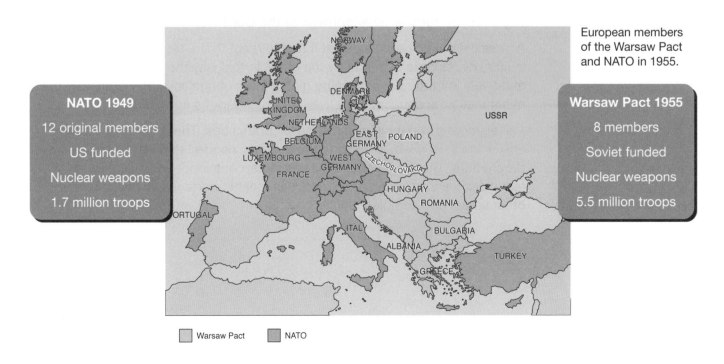

European members of the Warsaw Pact and NATO in 1955.

NATO 1949

12 original members

US funded

Nuclear weapons

1.7 million troops

Warsaw Pact 1955

8 members

Soviet funded

Nuclear weapons

5.5 million troops

Warsaw Pact ☐   NATO ☐

After the Warsaw Pact was formed, Khrushchev made a speech **denouncing** Stalin's legacy, and introducing **de-Stalinisation**. He seemed to be suggesting that a genuine 'Thaw' in Cold War relations was possible. Khrushchev appeared to be seeking **peaceful coexistence** between the superpowers.

Significance of NATO and the Warsaw Pact for the development of the Cold War

The formation of NATO and the Warsaw Pact effectively divided Europe, and most of the northern hemisphere, into two armed camps. Each could be a spark to light the nuclear powder keg.

Although officially defensive alliances, the formation of each worried the other side. This was especially the case when Stalin and Truman were no longer in charge. The new leaders (Khrushchev and Eisenhower) had new approaches, and both had a point to make.

The space race

Alongside weapons development (ICBM – intercontinental ballistic missile, and SLBM – submarine launched ballistic missile), both the USA and the USSR tried to outpace each other in space travel and technology. Rocket technology advanced dramatically, such that missiles could be fired from one superpower missile base to the opposition targets (ICBM). Submarines were difficult to monitor, so the threat of SLBM was psychologically challenging. The best known SLBM was the Polaris missile.

The military potential for a successful space mission was enormous. Both sides set about programmes to launch rockets with greater and greater potential. Ultimately, they both developed the ability to put humans in space. This technology was explored for military purposes, too, with the terrifying prospect that it may be possible to fire nuclear weapons from space one day.

Significance for the development of the Cold War

Across the period, each side felt it had to react to the technological and military developments made by the other. In this way the space race became massively important in advancing global fears of nuclear war. Control of space might mean the capacity to deliver nuclear weapons from space.

The economic impact was immense for both sides. The Americans had to ensure the public would support the tax rises needed to fund the space programme. The Soviet economy was state-controlled, and if limited resources went into the space race, this meant shortages in investment in other areas, for example industry.

The space race

1957 — **Sputnik** – First satellite put in orbit.

1957 — **Laika** – First animal in space (a dog).

1958 — **Explorer** – First communications satellite.

1961 — **Gagarin** – First human in space.

1961 — **Shepard** – First flight controlled by pilot.

1963 — **Tereshkova** – First woman in space.

1969 — **Armstrong** – First man on the Moon.

1971 — **Salyut** – First manned space station.

1975 — **Apollo-Soyuz** – First joint mission. This marked the end of the space race.

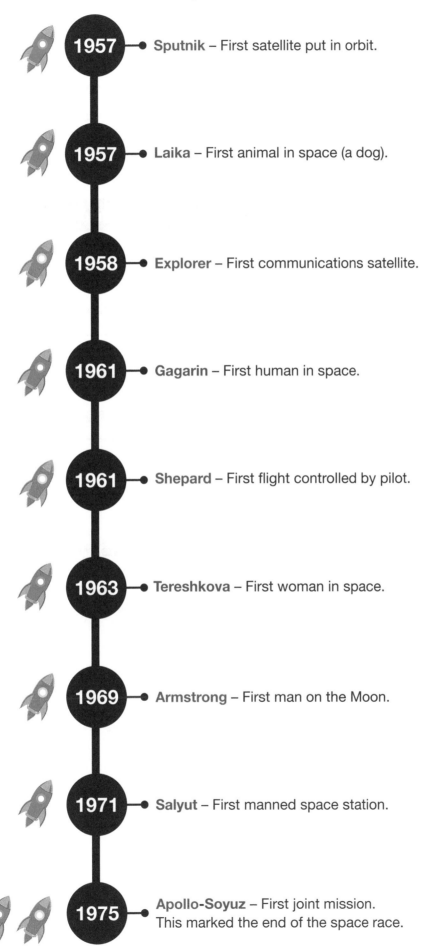

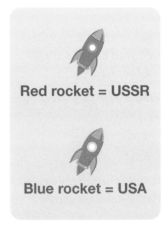

Red rocket = USSR

Blue rocket = USA

The Saturn IB rocket lifting off from Kennedy Space Centre with the USA's Apollo capsule in 1975.

The 'Thaw'

Hungary, the protest movement, and the reforms of Nagy

Like other countries in Eastern Europe, Hungary was ruled by a communist government, controlled by the USSR. Since 1949, the leader of Hungary had been Matyas Rakosi, a hard-line communist. Many Hungarians hated Rakosi's regime.

Rakosi's actions	Impact
Catholic leaders were arrested	People's religious beliefs were undermined
The Secret Police had the power to arrest people without trial	People were scared
Education followed the Soviet model	People were taught what communism demanded
Economy was poorly run, and heavy industry was outdated	People's living standards fell

Reasons why many Hungarians hated Rakosi's government.

Protesters took to the streets of Hungary's capital Budapest in October 1956.

After Stalin died in 1953, Nikita Khrushchev became Soviet leader. He appealed for 'peaceful co-existence' with the capitalist West. In 1956, protests in Poland against the communist government there gave Hungarians hope of reforms, as they believed there would be better relations between East and West, and this should lead to more democratic government.

Then in February 1956, Khrushchev made a speech denouncing the methods Stalin had used. He announced 'de-Stalinisation'. In Hungary, some people believed this meant they could replace their own leader, Rakosi, who used many of Stalin's methods to keep control.

Events of the Hungarian Uprising

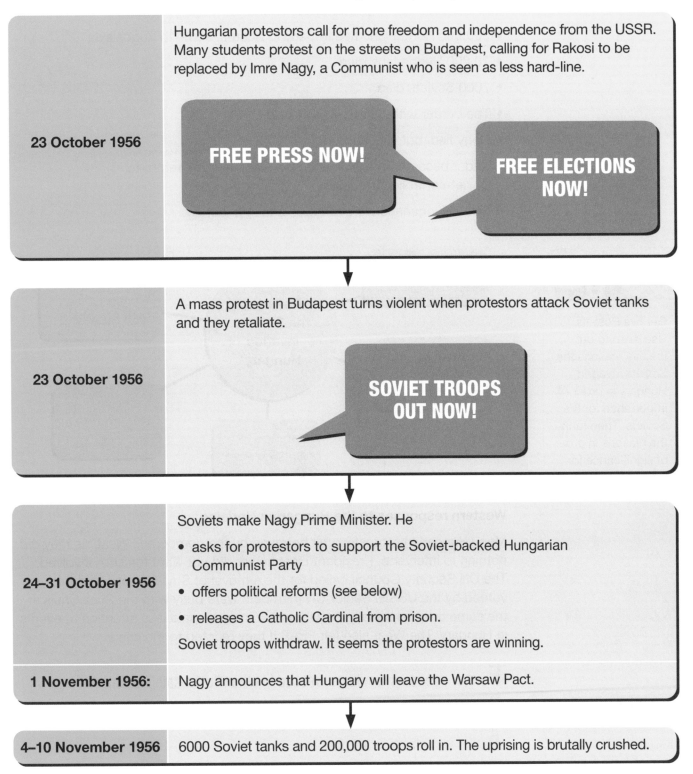

23 October 1956	Hungarian protestors call for more freedom and independence from the USSR. Many students protest on the streets on Budapest, calling for Rakosi to be replaced by Imre Nagy, a Communist who is seen as less hard-line. **FREE PRESS NOW!** **FREE ELECTIONS NOW!**
23 October 1956	A mass protest in Budapest turns violent when protestors attack Soviet tanks and they retaliate. **SOVIET TROOPS OUT NOW!**
24–31 October 1956	Soviets make Nagy Prime Minister. He • asks for protestors to support the Soviet-backed Hungarian Communist Party • offers political reforms (see below) • releases a Catholic Cardinal from prison. Soviet troops withdraw. It seems the protestors are winning.
1 November 1956:	Nagy announces that Hungary will leave the Warsaw Pact.
4–10 November 1956	6000 Soviet tanks and 200,000 troops roll in. The uprising is brutally crushed.

Nagy's reforms

- Freedom of speech and freedom to meet and protest
- Democracy introduced – political parties could be formed and elections would be held
- Secret police disbanded
- Political and religious prisoners would be freed

The following outcomes of the Hungarian Uprising and Soviet response to it meant the Soviets re-established control of Hungary:

- 200,000 Hungarians fled, mostly to Austria, some to Yugoslavia
- 20,000 Hungarians died
- 7000 Soviets died
- The border with Austria was closed
- Nagy fled, but was captured
- Kadar became Prime Minister: his rule marked a return to Soviet-controlled hardliners
- Many Hungarians were arrested and imprisoned.

Get five Post-its™. Use them to put the five reasons the Soviets invaded Hungary in order of importance for the Soviets. Then rank the reasons in order of significance for the development of the Cold War.

Western responses to the Hungarian Uprising

Many Hungarian protesters felt betrayed by the democratic West, as they did nothing to intervene. President Eisenhower did not want the USA involved. The UN Security Council called for the removal of Soviet troops, but this was vetoed by the USSR. Senior UN members were busy with the Suez Crisis at the same time (especially the UK and France) so paid less attention to events in Hungary. The West also felt FEAR if they reacted to the crisis:

Further freedoms would be crushed in other Soviet satellite states

End in a possible nuclear war

Action was also needed over Suez

Reaction of the Soviets and Chinese in other areas of conflict around the world

Reasons why the West did nothing to intervene in Hungary.

STRETCHIT!

A senior representative of the USSR was in Hungary in 1956 – Yuri Andropov. Research his career and his report dated 1 November 1956.

Significance of the Hungarian Uprising for the development of the Cold War

1 It confirmed that the USSR could act as they wished in its satellite states and the West was unlikely to do anything.

2 The limits of 'peaceful coexistence' between East and West had been defined by Khrushchev.

3 In the West, it led to growing mistrust of Khrushchev and heightened fears of the USSR.

The U2 crisis and its effects on the Paris Peace Summit and the peace process

After the uprising in Hungary, both sides were cautious, and some negotiations between the USSR and the USA began. However, hopes were literally shot out of the sky in May 1960.

The following events took place just two weeks before the scheduled Paris Peace Summit to discuss solutions to the division of Berlin.

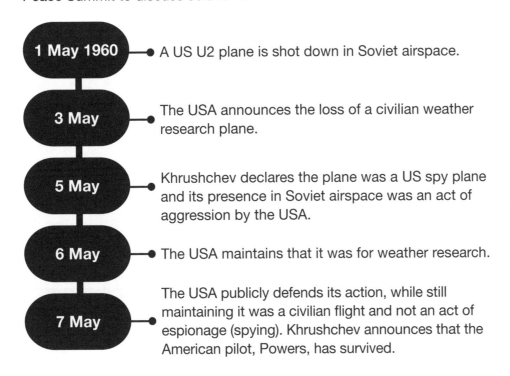

1 May 1960 — A US U2 plane is shot down in Soviet airspace.

3 May — The USA announces the loss of a civilian weather research plane.

5 May — Khrushchev declares the plane was a US spy plane and its presence in Soviet airspace was an act of aggression by the USA.

6 May — The USA maintains that it was for weather research.

7 May — The USA publicly defends its action, while still maintaining it was a civilian flight and not an act of espionage (spying). Khrushchev announces that the American pilot, Powers, has survived.

Pilot was Gary Powers

Observation and photography by a U2 plane

Weather research was claimed by the USA

Eisenhower ...

Refused to apologise for spying ...

Summit peace talks cancelled

NAIL IT!

It's easy to get confused between the Hungarian Uprising and the **Prague Spring**. Make sure you know what happened in each.

NAIL IT!

Memorise this POWERS acrostic to help you remember facts about the U2 crisis.

At the meeting before the Paris Peace Summit began:

1 Eisenhower admitted to Khrushchev that the U2 plane was spying, but he refused to apologise.

2 Khrushchev stormed out and cancelled the Paris Peace Summit. An invitation for Eisenhower to visit Moscow was withdrawn.

Powers was tried publicly in the Soviet Union, and sentenced to ten years for spying.

In November 1960, Eisenhower's presidency ended, and John F. Kennedy was elected as US President, partly on a promise to be hard on communism.

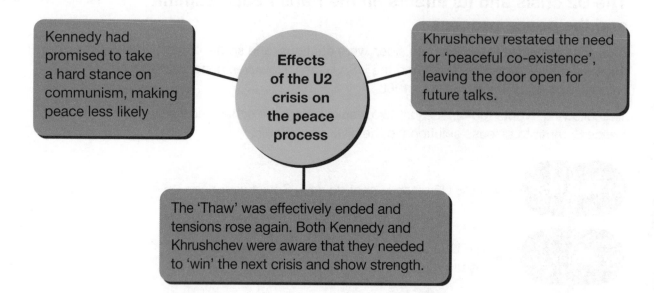

Kennedy had promised to take a hard stance on communism, making peace less likely

Effects of the U2 crisis on the peace process

Khrushchev restated the need for 'peaceful co-existence', leaving the door open for future talks.

The 'Thaw' was effectively ended and tensions rose again. Both Kennedy and Khrushchev were aware that they needed to 'win' the next crisis and show strength.

✓ CHECKIT!

1. List three consequences of Mao winning the civil war in China on the development of the Cold War.

2. Describe the Domino Theory?

3. Describe how the Viet Minh operated in South Vietnam.

4. Explain the rise in spending on nuclear weapons between 1949-53.

5. Describe the events after the formation of NATO that led to the Warsaw Pact being formed.

6. Who found the space race a greater drain on resources: the USA or the USSR? Why?

7. Explain why the West did not intervene more during the Soviet invasion of Hungary in 1956.

8. Create a 'FEAR' acrostic for the Soviets' concerns over Hungary.

Part Three:
Transformation of the Cold War

The Berlin Wall

DO IT!

Write a paragraph explaining why the Soviets wanted to stop people leaving the Soviet satellite states.

In the early hours of the morning on 13 August 1961, Soviet and East German soldiers put barbed wire barriers across the streets in Berlin. Three days later, they began to replace the barbed wire with a concrete wall. When they had finished, West Berlin was surrounded by a wall that was 4 metres high and 11 kilometres long. It was overlooked by armed border guards in over 300 watchtowers, who made sure nobody crossed.

Reasons for the construction of the Berlin Wall

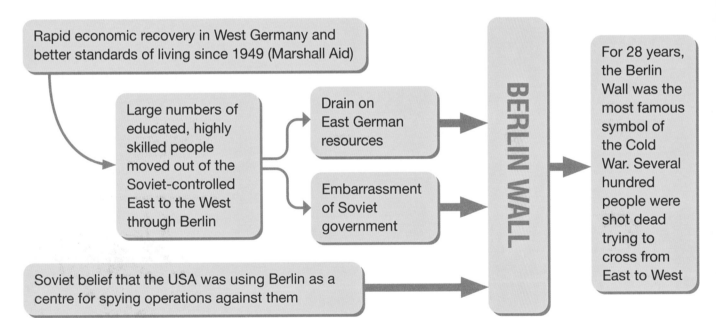

Rapid economic recovery in West Germany and better standards of living since 1949 (Marshall Aid)

Large numbers of educated, highly skilled people moved out of the Soviet-controlled East to the West through Berlin

Drain on East German resources

Embarrassment of Soviet government

Soviet belief that the USA was using Berlin as a centre for spying operations against them

BERLIN WALL

For 28 years, the Berlin Wall was the most famous symbol of the Cold War. Several hundred people were shot dead trying to cross from East to West

The building of the Berlin Wall, August 1961.

37

Today, in the world of freedom, the proudest boast is 'Ich bin ein Berliner'.

US President Kennedy giving his famous speech on 26 June 1963 in West Berlin.

President Kennedy's response

Nearly two years after the Soviets erected the wall, Kennedy visited West Berlin and spoke in front of a huge crowd. Germans living in West Berlin loved the speech, as it reinforced the view that the city was part of the West, and it gave people a sense of hope that they were not alone in the struggle against communism.

The USA used the Berlin Wall for propaganda, pointing out that they did not need to build a wall to keep their people in their country; this made the Soviets look bad in the eyes of people living in the West. However, the USA made no attempt to remove the wall. Kennedy said, 'a wall is better than a war'.

However, the two sides came very close to war on 27 October 1961, when US and Soviet tanks faced each other in a 'standoff' at Checkpoint Charlie (a well-known crossing point between East and West Berlin). Following an incident in which an American **diplomat** was refused entry by East German guards into East Berlin, a US army general ordered tanks to the checkpoint as a threat. The Soviet leader Nikita Khrushchev sent an equal number of tanks to face the Americans; they stood facing each other on either side of the checkpoint, some 75 metres apart, for 18 hours. Eventually, Kennedy was able to reach an agreement with Khrushchev and both sides backed down.

Berlin continued to be an area of tension, as East Germany remained cut off from West Germany and spying on both sides increased. However, it appeared that the USSR had given up trying to gain control of West Berlin. Therefore, the US policy of containment in Berlin had been successful.

Furthermore, by accepting the Wall, the West was in effect recognising East Germany. The Wall prevented the further drain of skilled workers to the West, allowing East Germany to develop economically. Stability had been provided.

STRETCH IT!

Watch the video of Kennedy's full speech. Why do you think this speech was so effective?

DO IT!

1 This cartoon is critical of the USSR. How can you tell?

2 Describe three or four features of the cartoon that suggest it is critical of the USSR.

3 Add one or two more pieces of information from your own knowledge that supports the message of the cartoon.

"See how many are staying on our side."

BERLIN WALL
ERECTED
AUG 13, 1961

An American cartoon published in 1961. It shows the Soviet leader Khrushchev looking over the Berlin Wall.

Tensions over Cuba

The island of Cuba lies just 160 km from the US state of Florida. Tensions over this island would lead to the Cuban Missile Crisis – the closest that the superpowers came to war.

In the 1950s, the USA was heavily involved in Cuba. American businessmen owned much of Cuba's industry, the military had a naval base there, and the US government supported the leader Batista, even though he was corrupt and unpopular with many Cubans.

Castro's revolution

After a three year struggle, in 1959 revolutionaries, led by Fidel Castro, overthrew Batista and set up a new Communist government. Despite supporting Castro at first, the US government was furious when many American businesses in Cuba were taken over by the new Cuban government. There were also thousands of Cubans who had fled to the USA, and they put pressure on the US government to act against Castro. As a result, the USA stopped trade with Cuba and President Eisenhower began to investigate ways of overthrowing Castro. Cuban refugees were provided with support and money, and some were trained to take part in a future invasion of Cuba. In the meantime, Cuba was suffering because the USA had banned all trade with it, so Cuba could no longer buy or sell goods with the USA. Castro asked Soviet leader Nikita Khrushchev for help, and the USSR began trading with Cuba.

The Bay of Pigs

In 1961, the new US President John F. Kennedy supplied weapons and transport for 1400 Cuban exiles to invade Cuba and overthrow Castro. In April, they landed at the Bay of Pigs in Cuba and were met by 20,000 Cuban troops armed with weapons supplied by the USSR. The Cubans quickly defeated the invaders. This was a humiliation for President Kennedy. It was clear the USA was behind the failed invasion and this drove Cuba into a closer alliance with the USSR. Relations between the USA and USSR were worse than ever.

The missile crisis

After the Bay of Pigs incident, Khrushchev gave Soviet military equipment to Castro, so he could prevent a further American invasion. The USA was worried about this. In September 1962, the Soviets reassured the USA they would not put nuclear missiles on Cuba. However, on 14 October 1962, two American U2 spy planes took photographs confirming the existence of missile bases there.

Fears of the USA and reaction to missiles on Cuba

The American public were outraged and afraid. The closeness of Cuba (see map below) meant that the weapons would take less than 20 minutes to destroy anywhere in the United States (except Alaska and Hawaii). The US government had several concerns:

- President Kennedy could not ignore public opinion, as elections for the US Congress were just a few weeks away; he needed to appear strong in response to what most Americans saw as Soviet aggression.

- Kennedy thought the Domino Theory had more chance of happening in South and Central America if the USA appeared weak in responding to the USSR placing missiles on Cuba. If more countries in the region became communist, that would seriously impact the US economy.

On 16 October, Kennedy called a meeting of the ExComm (Executive Committee of the National Security Council), where it was decided that the US government would take a tough approach to the developing crisis.

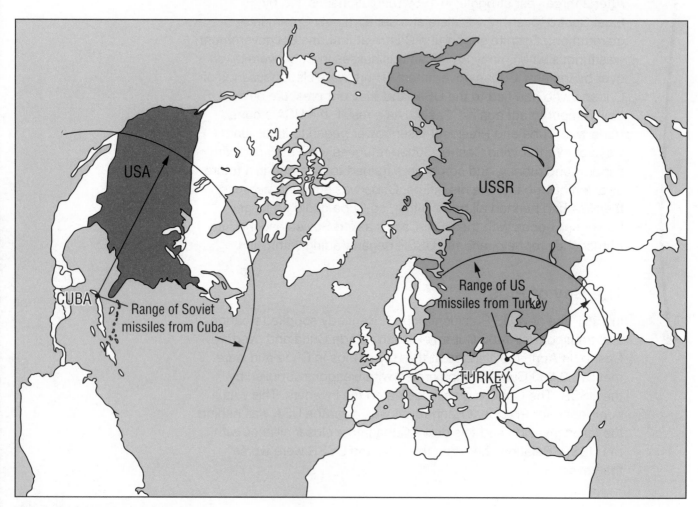

Map showing how far the destruction caused by nuclear weapons launched from Cuba and Turkey would reach.

Roles of Kennedy, Khrushchev and Castro

The aims and actions of these three men were hugely important before and during the missile crisis.

DO IT!

1 Summarise the aims of Kennedy, Khrushchev and Castro in a table.

2 As you read the timeline on the next page, complete your table by recording the actions taken by the three leaders.

Kennedy wanted to protect the USA and prevent countries from becoming communist. He also wanted Castro removed as Cuban leader and Cuba to become a US ally again. In November 1961, he launched a secret operation in Cuba called Operation Mongoose, where railways lines were blown up and sugar crops were poisoned.

Castro wanted to remain in power and protect Cuba. He appealed for Soviet help to do this after Operation Mongoose in 1961.

Khrushchev wanted to protect Cuba, the only communist country in the West. He also wanted Soviet missiles placed in Cuba to balance out the US missiles in Turkey. This would strengthen his negotiating position with the USA.

STRETCH IT!

When you have completed your table, write a paragraph to explain who you think did the most to increase tension during the Cuban Missile Crisis.

Events of the Cuban Missile Crisis

18 October 1962	The Soviet Foreign Minister denies there are any missiles in Cuba. **Kennedy** does not reveal that he knows about the missile bases spotted by the U2 planes.
22 October	**Kennedy** announces: • a naval blockade of Cuba, to stop any further missiles arriving there • that all missiles in Cuba should be removed.
24 October	Khrushchev orders the 20 Soviet ships heading for Cuba to ignore the US naval blockade.
25 October	The first Soviet ship, an oil tanker, is allowed through the blockade. The other ships are turned away by the blockade. Work on the missile bases in Cuba continues.
26 October	• **Castro** sends Khrushchev a private letter urging him to destroy the USA with nuclear weapons. • Kennedy considers an invasion of Cuba. It seems as though nuclear war is about to break out. • **Khrushchev** sends a private letter to Kennedy, offering to destroy the missile bases on Cuba if the USA publicly promises not to attack Cuba and lifts the blockade.
27 October	Shots are fired on both sides: • A US spy plane is shot down by a Soviet missile as it takes photographs over Cuba, killing the pilot. • A US navy destroyer ship near Cuba bombards a Soviet submarine, causing the crew to consider launching their nuclear missile. The submarine is forced to the surface, where US ships, from less than 20 metres away, fire shots across their bow. The Soviets turn for home. **Khrushchev** sends a second letter to Kennedy, stating that the USA must agree not to attack Cuba and remove its missiles from Turkey. Only then will the USSR remove its missiles from Cuba.
28 October	In order not to lose too much face, **Kennedy** replies to Krushchev's first letter publicly, agreeing to lift the naval blockade and promising not to invade Cuba. He replies secretly to Krushchev's second letter, agreeing to remove missiles from Turkey. An agreement is reached and **Khrushchev** publicly agrees to remove the Soviet missiles from Cuba.

Results of the crisis

The 13 days from 16 to 28 October 1962 were the closest the world had come to nuclear war.

- Both sides realised how easily war could break out and set up a telephone hotline, so that it would be easier for them to contact each other and settle their differences through talking.

- Kennedy looked like the 'winner', as he had stood up to the Soviets and they had backed down. His reputation improved even further following his speech in 1963 on 'a Strategy for Peace', calling for a ban on nuclear weapons testing.

- Cuba remained communist but no longer posed as much of a threat to the USA.

- Although Khrushchev might have been credited as the peacemaker, he was criticised within the USSR for appearing weak, as Kennedy's agreement to remove US missiles from Turkey had not been made public. Krushchev was sacked in 1964.

- Both sides continued developing weapons. By 1965, the USSR had caught up with the USA in the nuclear arms race; the two sides were now equal in terms of the weapons they could launch.

There were several treaties made between the USA and the USSR in the aftermath of the missile crisis:

- The Limited Test Ban Treaty (1963) limited the testing of nuclear weapons. While the treaty did not stop the development of nuclear weapons, it was a step forward.

- The 1967 Outer Space Treaty was an agreement between the USA and USSR 'to use outer space only for peaceful purposes'. In other words, there were to be no nuclear weapons launched from space or placed on the moon.

- In 1968, a Nuclear Non-Proliferation Treaty was signed. This aimed to prevent the spread of nuclear weapons to other countries.

DO IT!

'The Cuban Missile Crisis of 1962 actually helped to improve relations between East and West.' Write a paragraph to explain whether you agree or disagree with this statement and why.

STRETCH IT!

Write a balanced judgement to the 'Do it' question which both agrees and disagrees with the statement, using the phrases 'in the short term' and 'in the longer term'.

Czechoslovakia, 1968

Czechoslovakia, like other Soviet satellite states, was ruled by a Communist Party that was under Soviet control. By the mid-1960s, there were many social and economic problems in Czechoslovakia, and the Soviet-style economy was not providing solutions. Increasingly, people wanted change, but were frustrated at their lack of freedom to express their dissatisfaction with the communist regime.

Rights demanded	Reason
Political rights	There was no faith in the leader, Novotny, who was known to be taking money out of the system for his own use. He had not released political prisoners after Stalin's death, showing he remained a hardliner.
Consumer rights	There was no right to complain about poor quality goods.
Workers' rights	There was no incentive to work for state-controlled business, as wages were fixed.
People's rights	There was no way for people to voice their concerns.

Changes demanded in Czechoslovakia

DO IT!

Create a table with two headings: Novotny's Czechoslovakia up to 1968; Dubček's Czechoslovakia 1968. Under each heading match up the **problems** under Novotny with the **solutions** under Dubček.

Dubček and the Prague Spring movement

By 1968, the country was ripe for change. The Czechs had seen student demonstrations in Poland in March 1968. The Soviet leader, Brezhnev, removed Novotny and replaced him with Dubček as leader of Czechoslovakia. The Soviets felt Dubček would reduce the pressure for dramatic change and keep the Warsaw Pact from falling apart. They misjudged him.

Secret police activity was much reduced. Many political prisoners were released.

State control of business was ended and conditions improved for workers.

Dubček's actions during the Prague Spring

Dubček announced there would be multi-party elections in the future.

Movement beyond the Czech borders was allowed, meaning freedom to travel and to trade.

Freedom of speech and of meeting with others to discuss politics was allowed.

Press censorship was ended. This meant people could criticise the government.

Measures taken by Dubček during the Prague Spring.
He called it 'socialism with a human face'.

The USSR's response to Dubček's reforms

There were many issues and options for Brezhnev to consider before he responded to Dubček's reforms:

REMEMBER HUNGARY..

To learn from the actions of Khrushchev in Hungary in 1956.

To keep Soviet influence in Czechoslovakia.

To stop unrest spreading to other Soviet satellite states.

To keep the Warsaw Pact together.

To stop Tito and Yugoslavia from gaining support in Eastern Europe.

Options for Brezhnev in the Prague Spring

P revent change in Czechoslovakia?

How?

R oll in the Warsaw Pact tanks?

OR

A ccept change in Czechoslovakia?

How?

G ive Dubček more freedom to act.

EITHER WAY

U ncertainty would surely lead to ...

E scalation of the problems for Brezhnev and the Soviets.

NAILIT!

Learn the acrostic of options for Brezhnev in the Prague Spring.

45

STRETCHIT!

Remember that the Prague Spring took place 12 years after the Hungarian Uprising. Media coverage of foreign events had improved a lot in that time, which meant the West knew all that was going on there. This increased public pressure on the West to act to support Czechoslovakia.

Actions of Brezhnev

The Warsaw Pact countries met without Czechoslovakia and discussed what to do. In June and July 1968, members of the Warsaw Pact carried out military exercises on the Czech border. The Warsaw Pact sent the 'Warsaw letter' to Dubček, stating that all members had the right to self-determination, but the unity of the communist system was more important. Brezhnev then met Dubček, who refused to stop his reforms.

On 3 August, the 'Bratislava Declaration' of unity was signed by Dubček. It seemed to calm the situation, as it declared Czech faith in communism. Then on 9 August, Dubček met Yugoslavia's Tito. However, Tito was distrusted by Moscow, so this led, on 18 August, to Brezhnev raging at Dubček over the phone.

On 20 and 21 August, Soviet forces crushed the street protests in Czech cities, including Prague. Dubček was forced to reverse his reforms and resigned as Czech leader. The bloody street battles took a heavy toll: 500 civilians were wounded and around 100 killed. A new hard line Communist government was established.

Impact on relations between East and West

The Soviet invasion of Czechoslovakia deepened tension between the superpowers, as well as within the blocs themselves.

STRETCHIT!

List as many similarities and differences as possible between the causes, events and consequences of Hungary 1956 and Czechoslovakia 1968. Rank them by significance of impact on tension between East and West.

Warsaw **P**act governments were fearful of Soviet intervention in their countries

Anti-Communists in Eastern European countries feared violence against them

China was outraged

Troops returning home to the USSR told families that they were not supported by the people of Czechoslovakia

Western action depended on US and UN policy not to intervene behind the Iron Curtain

Events in Vietnam made the USA nervous

Soviet veto blocked a UN resolution condemning the violence

Talks between Brezhnev and Johnson were cancelled

NAILIT!

Remember to consider different groups within the Eastern Bloc. Yugoslavia's ability to act independently, for instance, damaged the image of complete Soviet control. Remember you are looking at effects within each bloc, and between them.

Brezhnev Doctrine

Determined to avoid anything like the Prague Spring happening again, Brezhnev announced the Brezhnev Doctrine in November 1968.

USSR will keep Communists in power in Europe and elsewhere

Internal rebellions will be crushed

External invasion will be met by force

NAILIT!

Three other elements to bear in mind when considering the Brezhnev Doctrine:

- China worried about Soviet intervention during the Cultural Revolution.

- The USA realised the Doctrine was defensive, not expansionist, and so not aimed at the West.

- The doctrine was announced as Richard Nixon, known for being anti-communist, became US President.

Easing of tension

There were two major sources of superpower tension in the late 1960s.

1 **Vietnam War**

2 **Soviet record on human rights**

Year	Number killed	Total casualties
1966	5000	35,000
1967	9000	65,000
1968	14,500	103,000
1969	9000	62,000
1970	4000	29,000

US casualties in Vietnam (Numbers rounded. Casualties includes killed, wounded and missing.)

Vietnam

As we saw on page 26, President Johnson hugely increased the American military presence in Vietnam once he became president in 1963. The aim was to prevent South Vietnam becoming communist. By 1968, there were 500,000 US troops in Vietnam. The economic cost was huge and unsustainable. The human cost was terrible, as hundreds of thousands of American troops and Vietnamese fighters and civilians lost their lives or were badly injured.

The war became increasingly unpopular with the American public because of the high numbers of casualties and the tactics used. It was also becoming obvious that Vietnam was a war that the United States could not win. Presidents Johnson and Nixon both vowed to end the Vietnam War, but neither could accept defeat: to do so would mean victory for communism, and therefore disaster in a US presidential election.

Soviet record on human rights

The Soviet leadership had occasionally eased up on restrictions – the period of the 'Thaw' for example – but had largely clamped down on the sorts of rights demanded in Hungary and Czechoslovakia.

The US government criticised the Soviets' record on human rights. For example, the terrible conditions in work camps ('Gulags') for political prisoners were widely publicised and criticised outside the USSR – but not within it, of course, due to censorship. However, the Americans did not allow poor human rights in many of the communist states to stand in the way of peace.

The reasons for Détente

Détente was an attempt to reduce tension by both the USA and the USSR. Under détente, the idea of climbing down from the edge of a nuclear nightmare was explored. The difficulty would come over who would remove their nuclear weapons first, but both sides had good reasons to seek détente.

DO IT!

Write three sentences to explain why US actions in Vietnam in 1968 can be seen as a disaster.

Both sides wanted Détente because:	The USA wanted Détente because:	The USSR want Détente because:
• They were shocked by how close the Cold War had come to nuclear war during the Cuban Missile Crisis. • Building and maintaining nuclear weapons was very expensive.	• The financial and human costs of the Vietnam War were very high, with both money and American lives. • The war was increasingly unpopular with the American public. • Nixon wanted to improve relations with China.	• Supporting communist regimes across the globe was very expensive and the Soviet economy was overstretched • Nixon's advances to China worried Brezhnev.

After the Cuban Missile Crisis, both sides realised the need for Détente. In 1963 the Limited Nuclear Test Ban Treaty was signed and the 'hotline' between Moscow and Washington was set up. In 1969 both East and West Germany agreed not to develop nuclear weapons.

SALT 1

Strategic Arms Limitations Talks (SALT) were formal meetings between the superpowers, which began in November 1969. Three treaties were signed:

- The Anti-Ballistic Missile Treaty limited anti-ballistic nuclear weapons to 200 each.

- The Interim Treaty limited numbers of ICBMs. The Soviets had more, but the USA had more strategic bombers.

- In the Basic Principles Treaty, the USA and the USSR pledged 'to do their utmost to avoid military confrontation' and 'to exercise restraint' in international relations.

These treaties were signed by Brezhnev and Nixon in Moscow, in May 1972, after Nixon had visited China. Nixon's visit to China had worried the Soviets into action. When Nixon was re-elected US President in 1972, plans began for SALT 2. Brezhnev had consolidated his position. The role of the two leaders was front page news, and allowed the world to believe a nuclear war could be avoided.

STRETCHIT!

The agreement between East and West Germany not to develop nuclear weapons was part of Ostpolitik, the brainchild of Willy Brandt. He was the Chancellor of West Germany, and pushed the thawing of economic relations between East and West in Europe. Research Ostpolitik and Brandt. Consider the significance of these actions.

CHECK IT!

1. Give two reasons why people in Eastern Europe wanted to move to the West through West Berlin.

2. Give two reasons why the Berlin Wall was constructed.

3. Explain why building the wall increased tension between the two superpowers.

4. Give a long-, medium-, and short-term cause of the Cuban Missile Crisis.

5. List the rights some Czechs wanted that led to the Prague Spring.

6. What did the Brezhnev Doctrine state?

7. What was the biggest source of tension between the superpowers in the late 1960s? Why?

8. Explain the main reasons for Détente.

How to answer the exam questions

Question 1: Source analysis

About the question

 AQA exam-style question

> Source A supports/opposes/is critical of … How do you know?
>
> Explain your answer using **Source A** and your contextual knowledge.
>
> **4 marks**

This question is asking you to analyse sources contemporary to the period (AO3). You will need to make inferences about the message of the source and use contextual knowledge to help explain the point the artist is trying to make. The source will be in a separate source booklet. It will usually be a cartoon or a poster, and information about the source will be given in the caption.

As this question is only worth 4 marks, you only need to write a short paragraph to answer it – be concise and focused. Take around 5 minutes to answer this question in the exam.

According to the mark scheme:

- Answers that don't get any marks will fail to answer the question or describe a feature of the source.

- Level 1 (1–2 marks) answers will describe a feature of the source and support this with some knowledge.

- Level 2 (3–4 marks) answers will describe a feature of the source and analyse how the source supports/opposes/is critical of whatever is stated in the question. The answer will be supported by knowledge that is related to the feature described.

Answering the question

It might be useful to take a step-by-step approach to answering the question.

Step 1

Describe one or two **key features** of the image that suggests the artist supports or is critical of whatever is in the question.

Key features are the people and objects and how they are shown, for example their facial expressions or body language, or words that appear within the image or as a caption. Everything has been included and positioned where it is for a reason.

Step 2

Explain the **inference** the key feature/s is making. How does the key feature suggest that the artist supports or is critical of the country or person stated in the exam question?

An **inference** is what is implied by the key feature rather than what is explicitly shown; in other words, what message the source is giving.

Step 3

Use **contextual knowledge** to support the message of the image.

Contextual knowledge is information that you have about what was going on at the time the image was produced. You should provide one or two facts that help explain the artist's message.

NAILIT!

The mark scheme asks for 'Developed analysis of source based on content and/ or provenance'. Note the and/or – this means that you do not need to do both!

Source A An American cartoon on the Berlin Blockade called 'How to close the gap?', published in 1948.

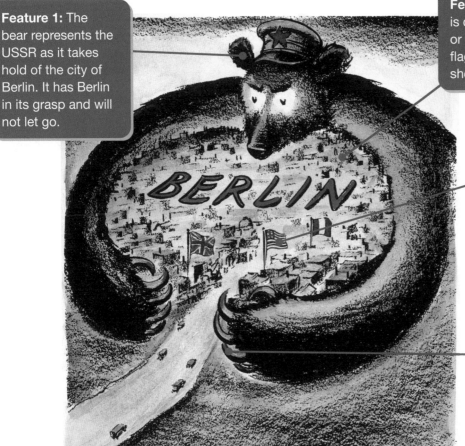

Feature 1: The bear represents the USSR as it takes hold of the city of Berlin. It has Berlin in its grasp and will not let go.

Feature 2: The city is coloured grey or black, while the flags of the allies are shown in colour.

Feature 3: The flags of the Western allies are drawn close together near the entrance of the city.

Feature 4: The bear's claws are dripping with blood.

It will be possible to make several inferences from any source. The table below contains some inferences from Source A.

A This represents the zones dividing Berlin after the war and the closeness here shows that the allies were working together.		C This symbolises the communist influence in the city and that the goal of the allies was to stand up against and contain communism.	
B This represents the blockade of Berlin, when the Soviets cut off supply routes so that Berlin would become reliant on the USSR and the Western powers could be driven out.		D This shows that the cartoonist thinks the USSR is dangerous and poses a real threat.	

1 Which features labelled in Source A could you use to support each inference in the table above? Complete the table above with the correct detail number.

2 What inference can be drawn from the cartoon being called 'How to close the gap'?

3 Pictures are a memorable way of recalling information. Draw a copy of Source A and annotate it with contextual information on the topic (the Berlin Blockade).

NAILIT!

Remember to study all aspects of the cartoon: including

- the caption (above the picture in the sources booklet)
- any writing within the picture
- the background as well as the foreground in the picture
- the date and place it was published.

AQA exam-style question

Study **Source B**.

Source B is critical of the USA. How do you know?

Explain your answer using **Source B** and your contextual knowledge

4 marks

Source B On 29 October 1945, President Truman made a speech on 12 points about US foreign policy. This cartoon appeared in a British newspaper the following day.

Key feature: US President Truman is shown holding the atom bomb under his arm; it is labelled 'private'.

Inference: This is critical of the USA because it suggests that Truman is not sharing information with his allies. Although Truman suggests that he wants to work with the UK and the USSR with mutual trust, he does not want to share nuclear technology. This is causing tension with the Russian and British leaders, which is shown by their facial expressions.

Contextual knowledge: The USA dropped atom bombs on Japan to bring the Second World War to an end in August 1945. The USA thought that the atom bomb had been kept secret up until the Potsdam Conference, but the Russians knew about the weapon and were suspicious as to why the Americans wanted to keep it secret. By October 1945, the USA was still unwilling to share the new weapons technology with those who were supposed to be its allies.

"WHY CAN'T WE WORK TOGETHER IN MUTUAL TRUST & CONFIDENCE?"

Sample answer

The answer uses source analysis to explain how Source B shows it is critical of the USA.

Key features of the source that show it is critical of the USA are described.

The student has used knowledge of the historical context in which the source is created to support their analysis.

The cartoon is critical of the USA because it shows the American President saying one thing while doing another. President Truman is shown holding an atom bomb that is labelled 'private' while asking the other leaders 'why can't we work together in mutual trust and confidence?' but Attlee and Stalin look suspicious. This shows that Truman wanted Attlee and Stalin to trust him but did not want to share the technology so they could make their own bombs. The USA did not tell its allies that it had made the atom bomb, which was tested the day before the Potsdam Conference and dropped on Japan in August. This cartoon is from October 1945, and by this time the USA had not shared the secrets of the making of the atom bomb, which increased tension between East and West.

DO IT!

What level do you think this sample answer would be given according to the mark scheme below?

- Answers that don't get any marks will fail to answer the question or describe a feature of the source.

- Level 1 (1–2 marks) answers will describe a feature of source and support this with some knowledge.

- Level 2 (3–4 marks) answers will describe a feature of the source and analyse how the source supports/opposes/is critical of whatever is stated in the question. The answer will be supported by knowledge that is related to the feature described.

Question 2: How useful are sources …

About the question

AQA exam-style question

How useful are **Sources B** and **C** to a historian studying …

Explain your answer using **Sources B** and **C** and your contextual knowledge.

12 marks

This question is about evaluating the usefulness of two sources for a given enquiry. You will never be given a source that is completely useless for the topic, but some sources will be more useful than others depending on their provenance and content. You need to evaluate the content and provenance of the sources using your own knowledge.

- **Provenance** means thinking about the 5Ws – Who, What, Where, When, Why. Who created the source? What type of source is it? And when, where and why was the source produced?

- **Content** means the points being made in the source or what the source can tell us.

- **Contextual knowledge** means bringing relevant knowledge you have to test the provenance and content of the sources.

This question is worth 12 marks, so it's important to spend enough time on it in the exam – around 18 minutes. Aim to write three developed paragraphs: one paragraph on Source B and another on Source C (these should tell us how useful each source is for the topic being studied), and a third paragraph that deals with the sources together. Your answer should reach a substantiated judgement on exactly how useful the sources are *for the topic studied*.

According to the mark scheme:

- Answers that don't get any marks will fail to answer the question at all.

- Level 1 answers (1–3 marks) will describe basic features of one or both sources that are related to the given enquiry.

- Level 2 answers (4–6 marks) will show some basic source analysis of the content and/or provenance of both sources.

- Level 3 answers (7–9 marks) will evaluate the usefulness of the sources, giving reasons based on their content and/or provenance.

- Level 4 answers (10–12 marks) will evaluate the usefulness of both sources using both their content and provenance. They might evaluate the relationship between the sources and how this makes them more or less useful.

NAILIT!

Consider using **P.C. O'Knowledge**, the History Copper, to help you remember **P**rovenance, **C**ontent and **O**wn **K**nowledge when answering this question.

55

To give yourself the best chance to achieve the top marks, you need to:

- cover **BOTH sources**

- answer the **TOPIC raised** in the question (the **topic** is at the end – the knowledge aspect)

- use reasoning to **EVALUATE** how useful each source is. This should be based on BOTH the content and the provenance of the sources.

If you attempt these, but don't manage them well, you may drop into level 3, or even level 2; but without them, you cannot get to level 4.

Answering the question

One way of planning your answer to this question is to take a step-by-step approach. Read the following exam question and sources.

AQA exam-style question

Study **Sources C** and **D**.

How useful are **Sources C** and **D** to a historian studying opinions of the nuclear arms race?

Explain your answer using **Sources C** and **D** and your contextual knowledge.

12 marks

Source C From a book *Common Sense and Nuclear Warfare* published in 1959. It was written by Bertrand Russell, a British philosopher and well-known anti-nuclear campaigner. John Dulles was US Secretary of State (head of foreign policy).

Since the nuclear stalemate became apparent, the governments of East and West have adopted the policy which Mr. Dulles calls 'brinkmanship'. This is a policy adapted from a sport which, I am told, is practiced by some youthful degenerates. This sport is called 'Chicken!' It is played by choosing a long straight road ... and starting two very fast cars towards each other from opposite ends ... As they approach each other, mutual destruction becomes more and more imminent ...

Before analysing Sources C and D, record a simple gut-feeling judgement on how useful you think each will be for the task at hand. Even a simple mark out of 5 would help. You can revisit your initial judgement after analysis.

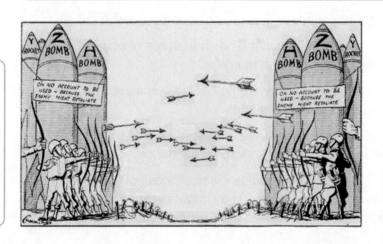

Source D A cartoon by a British cartoonist, Cummings, in a British newspaper, August 1953. By this time, the world was aware that both sides had developed hydrogen bombs.

Step 1 – Topic of enquiry

It's important to identify what enquiry the sources will be used for, because the usefulness of a source depends on this. A source may be extremely useful for one enquiry but not very useful for another. In the exam question above, the topic is 'opinions of the nuclear arms race'. That is very different from another enquiry such as 'events of the arms race' or 'policies of the US and Soviet governments on nuclear weapons'.

Step 2 – Provenance

For each source, think about the 5Ws (see page 55). You won't need all of these, just the crucial ones for your argument. You can get much of this information from the caption.

The table below gives the 5Ws for Source C. Usually you will need to work out the answer to 'why' the source was created from the other Ws. In this case, because it was written by a well-known anti-nuclear campaigner in 1959, we can surmise that he wrote the book to give the reasons for his views and to try to persuade other people that his view is correct, so they can pressurise governments to stop the arms race.

DO IT!

Complete the table for Source D.

	Who?	What?	Where?	When?	Why?
Source C	Bertrand Russell – British philosopher and anti-nuclear campaigner	A book	Unknown – probably in Britain, though available worldwide	1959	To explain his anti-nuclear views and try to convince others that his view is correct
Source D					

Step 3 – Content

Give three points made in the source related to the topic in the question.

Step 4 – Own knowledge

Give three points you want to make from your own knowledge about the topic in the question.

Step 5: Identify information you will use.

Remember that you don't need to use all the information you have in your plan.

For steps 3 and 4 you could create a spider diagram such as the one on the next page. For step 5 you could circle or underline the pieces of information you will use next in your answer.

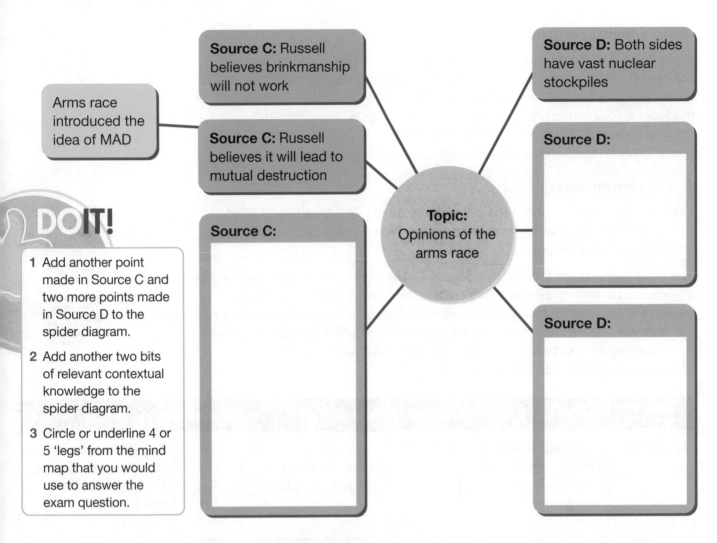

Arms race introduced the idea of MAD

Source C: Russell believes brinkmanship will not work

Source C: Russell believes it will lead to mutual destruction

Source C:

Topic: Opinions of the arms race

Source D: Both sides have vast nuclear stockpiles

Source D:

Source D:

DO IT!

1 Add another point made in Source C and two more points made in Source D to the spider diagram.

2 Add another two bits of relevant contextual knowledge to the spider diagram.

3 Circle or underline 4 or 5 'legs' from the mind map that you would use to answer the exam question.

Step 6 – Explain usefulness

Add a brief comment on **how** the information you have given from each source is **useful** in studying the topic in the question. You could also add another comment on how both sources, if taken together, are useful for studying the topic. For example, see how this has been done for Source C and both sources below.

DO IT!

Complete the summary of how useful Source D is for this topic.

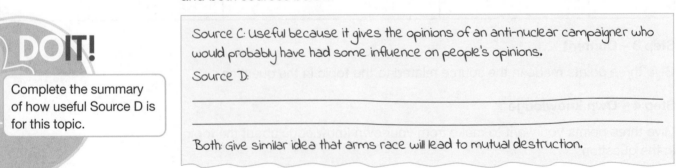

Source C: useful because it gives the opinions of an anti-nuclear campaigner who would probably have had some influence on people's opinions.

Source D:

_____

_____

Both: Give similar idea that arms race will lead to mutual destruction.

Step 7 – Write your answer.

Sample answer

AQA exam-style question

Study **Sources E** and **F**.

How useful are **Sources E** and **F** to a historian studying China's role in the Korean War?

Explain your answer using **Sources E** and **F** and your contextual knowledge.

12 marks

Source E General Bradley, a senior US army officer, speaking to the US senate in 1951, during the MacArthur hearings into MacArthur's dismissal. Although he worked alongside MacArthur, Bradley's testimony helped Truman's government sack MacArthur.

The strategic alternative, enlargement of the war in Korea to include Red China, would probably delight the Kremlin [the Soviet government] more than anything else we could do. It would necessarily tie down additional forces, especially our sea power and our air power, while the Soviet Union would not be obliged to put a single man in the conflict. Under present circumstances, we have recommended against enlarging the war. The course of action often described as a 'limited war' with Red China would increase the risk we are taking by engaging too much of our power in an area that is not the strategic prize.

Source F. A Chinese enlistment poster for the Korean War created by the communist government to recruit soldiers to fight in Korea.

DO IT!

Look back at the mark scheme on page 55. What level would you give the student's answer on the next page?

Before looking at their sample answer to this question, here is the plan a student created.

<1>China's role in Korean war

<2> Source E - who: General Bradley senior army officer/what: Speech/where: US senate/when: 1951 during MacArthur Hearings/why: Giving evidence to senate

Source F - who: Chinese govt/what: poster/where: China/when: 1951/why: Propaganda

<3> Source E - (1) MacArthur's plan was not agreed with by all his Generals. (2) Bradley is concerned more with the USSR than with China. (3) War with China would be difficult and costly in manpower and resources.

Source F - (1) China portrays itself as a peaceful (dove). (2) Planes show high tech will be used. (3) USA will suffer heavy losses.

<4> (1) China supported communist North Korea. (2) China was used to warfare in Asian surroundings - Civil war. (3) The USSR had nuclear technology by this time, and supported the Chinese.

<5> Points to use circled.

<6> The poster helps show China's approach and determination. Hearings into dismissal helps see how US actions were affected by China's role but Bradley being more concerned with the USSR helps keep China's role in perspective. The USSR were behind China, and China supporting communist North Korea helps cement the importance of the role played by China.

The student used the plan above to write the following answer.

The answer is well structured, covering both sources in separate paragraphs and with a final concluding paragraph on both sources.

Source E is useful for a historian studying China's role in the Korean war because it is from the official hearings into General MacArthur's actions. I know he took his army to within 80km of the Chinese border, and threatened to invade. He also wanted to use nuclear weapons against China. So, it is useful to see China's influence in shaping American actions in Korea. It is also useful to show that a senior General, Bradley, still considered the USSR as the major threat to American aims in the Cold war, but was aware that the Chinese role could demand a heavy price from American soldiers and resources.

The provenance of each source is also used to help explain how useful it is.

Each source is evaluated against the student's own contextual knowledge.

Source F is also useful in studying China's role in the Korean war because it is from the Chinese communist government during the war. It shows China as the dove of peace in the war. The planes suggest advanced technology will be used, which would be more attractive to soldiers than fighting in the fields. It also shows that the Chinese Red Army will destroy the USA, as shown by the crosses. This shows the importance of China's role in supporting North Korea, as their limitless supply of men and machines would stop the USA from winning a quick victory. The USSR was behind the technological ability of China. I also know North Korea was dependant on Chinese support to continue the war. It is useful, as it shows the difference in Chinese and American approaches to the war.

The student explains how each source's content is useful for the enquiry. Note the technique of 'useful... China's role in the Korean War....because'.

Both these sources are useful when studying China's role in the Korean war because, taken together, they show how far apart the two sides were during the war in Korea. They show us different perspectives on the Korean war, and on how significant the Chinese role was at this time. While F is recruitment poster, and E is under oath at a hearing, and might therefore appear more useful, they both present assessments of the strength of China's role as it was perceived within the two camps.

The usefulness of both sources together is also considered.

Question 3: Write an account …

About the question

AQA exam-style question

> Write an account of how … became an international crisis/increased Cold War tensions …
>
> **8 marks**

This question is about explaining how one event caused an international crisis or an increase in Cold War tensions. It requires you to show your knowledge and understanding of **chronology** as well as **cause and consequence**.

- **Chronology** means studying events in date order. How will you use the events to support your analysis of cause and consequence?

- **Cause and consequence** means the reasons an event happened and the results of the event. In this case, the result is always either an international crisis or an increase in Cold War tensions. How will you be sure to add analysis to the chronology?

You will need to write a coherent narrative – probably two paragraphs in 12 minutes. In each paragraph you **must show how an event led to escalation on an international level**.

You will be marked according to the following Assessment Objectives:

- AO1: demonstrate knowledge and understanding of the key features and characteristics of the period studied.

- AO2: Explain and analyse historical events and periods studied using second-order historical concepts.

According to the mark scheme:

- Answers that don't get any marks fail to answer the question.

- Level 1 answers (1–2 marks) will give some basic statements of causes and/or consequences of events.

- Level 2 answers (3–4 marks) will give some reasons for causes and/or consequences of events supported with factual knowledge.

- Level 3 answers (5–6 marks) will give more reasons for why things happened, supported with a range of factual knowledge.

- Level 4 answers (7–8 marks) will give a range of reasons for why things happened, supported with detailed factual knowledge.

To maximise your chance of hitting level 4, there should be at least **TWO causes or consequences** discussed. ONE would limit the outcome to level 3, at best. In both cases, you must address the **TOPIC** in the question.

'Telling the story' without analysing cause or consequence will limit you to levels 1 and 2.

NAILIT!

Remember to tie your causes and consequences to the focus of the question – the **escalation to an international crisis** or **increased tension.** This is the key element to climbing the levels.

Answering the question

Again, let's work through answering this question using a step-by-step approach. Read the following question.

AQA exam-style question

Write an account of how events in Cuba in 1962 became an international crisis.

8 marks

Step 1

'Brain dump' the events you know for the year and place in the question.

For this question you need to list events in 1962 or related to Cuba. Don't write more than ten things, as you would be using up too much valuable time.

Step 2

Use a highlighter to select 6 or 7 of the most important points. Alternatively, cross out the points you won't use.

Step 3

Add dates to the highlighted points, so you know the order in which you need to write about them.

Steps 1, 2 and 3 have been partially completed below.

Step 4

Decide how much tension each event you have chosen added.

One way to do this is to grade each event out of five, where one is for something that added little tension and five greatly increased tension.

DO IT!

1 Add five more events to complete step 1.

2 Highlight the most important events.

3 Add dates to these events.

4 Grade the highlighted events from 1–5, depending on how much tension they added.

USSR put missiles in Cuba ... Summer, 1962

Soviet Foreign Minister denied there were missiles in Cuba ... 18 October

Kennedy announced that all missiles in Cuba should be removed ... 22 October

Soviet ships heading for Cuba were turned around by the blockade ... 24 October

Step 5

Plan your paragraphs. Aim to write two.

You could use a flow chart to **sequence** your answer, to show some of the consequences of each of the main events. This might be a link to another event or it could be the reactions or thoughts of people/governments. Use words and phrases such as *consequently, this meant that, this led to, as a result* in the right-hand boxes.

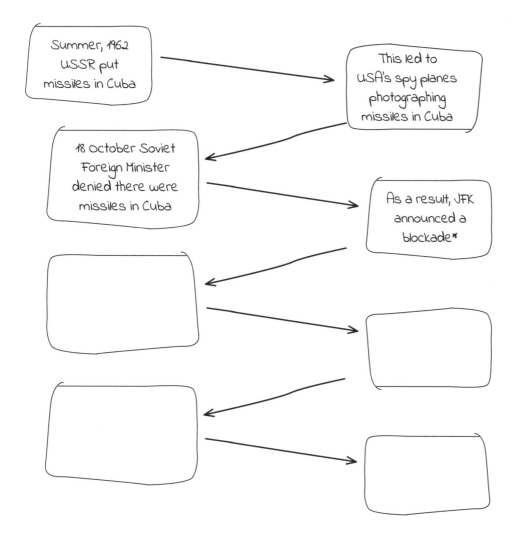

Step 6

Identify where you will address '**became an international crisis**'. Put an asterisk (*) next to at least two events that you graded '5'.

This is a matter of deciding which events were most important in raising the level of tension. These will be the events that you focus much of your answer on.

Step 7

Write your answer!

DO IT!

1 Complete the flow chart with all the events in the left-hand boxes. In the right-hand boxes, build your links between events, using *consequently, this meant that, this led to, as a result.*

2 Identify the other event that you think most increased tensions so it became an international crisis by putting an asterisk next to it.

Sample answer

AQA exam-style question

Write an account of how events in Berlin led to an international crisis in 1948.

8 marks

Before looking at a sample answer to this question, let's look at how a student has used the step-by-step approach in a slightly different way to the previous page to plan their answer.

West combined zones - August 1948

~~Formation of West and East Germany - 1949~~

Marshall Aid in West Berlin - early 1948

Deutsche Mark - June

Economic recovery in West Berlin - throughout 1948 ⑤

Poverty in eastern Germany + Berlin - throughout 1948 ⑤

Berlin Blockade - roads, railways and canals - 24 June ⑤

~~Blockade ended - May 1949~~

Berlin Airlift - supplied West Berlin - 26 June 1948-30 Sept 1949

~~Creation of NATO - 1949~~

Paragraph 1 on Marshall Aid - angered Stalin (dollar imperialism) + Deutsche Mark - led to W. German economic recovery - added to Soviet fears as many left East for West - led to Stalin wanting to rid Berlin of western powers

Paragraph 2 on Blockading Berlin - led to increased tensions and possibility of armed conflict, as some in USA wanted to attack - Truman chose airlift - kept tensions high, as possible that USSR would attack US planes

The student used the plan on the previous page to write the following answer:

One way in which events in Berlin led to an international crisis in 1948 was when western parts of Germany and West Berlin received Marshall Aid. This angered Stalin, as he thought Marshall Aid was the USA's way of trying to take over countries through its money. In June, the British and USA, which had combined their zones of Germany in 1947, introduced a new currency, the Deutsche Mark, in their combined zone. As a result of these actions by the west, the economy of West Germany and West Berlin started to recover, while East Germany and East Berlin still had many economic problems. People living in the East saw that life in the west was better, because West Berlin was right in the middle of the Soviet zone of Germany so many people left the East for the West. Consequently, the actions of the west, which helped West Berlin prosper, angered and worried Stalin and so he wanted the western powers out of Berlin altogether, which heightened tensions between both sides.

A second way was when Stalin responded to these events by blockading West Berlin. This meant that access to West Berlin by roads, railways and canals was stopped, effectively cutting off West Berlin from West Germany. The blockade angered US President Truman and other western powers because they wanted to maintain their influence in West Berlin. The blockade greatly heightened tensions between East and West and as a result caused an international crisis. This was because some in the west wanted to attack the USSR or East Germany, but Truman decided on a different action - the Berlin Airlift. This was where West Berlin was supplied with food and other things by American aircraft. As a result, more tension was caused, because nobody knew if the USSR would attack the US planes.

> Events are written about in chronological order, which shows knowledge and understanding.

> Detailed factual knowledge of the events are shown.

> The answer shows analysis of how each event led to an international crisis.

DO IT!

1 Circle parts of the student's answer to show where phrases such as *consequently, this meant that, this led to, as a result* are used. Is there at least one in each paragraph? Are they linked to '**led to an international crisis**'?

2 Look back at the mark scheme on page 61. What level would this student's answer achieve?

Question 4: Essay question

About the question

AQA exam-style question

> 'The main reason for … was …'
>
> How far do you agree with this statement?
>
> Explain your answer.
>
> **(16 marks + 4 SPaG)**

This question asks about the reasons/causes of key events and requires an extended answer. It is worth 16 marks, plus 4 extra marks for Spelling, Punctuation and Grammar (SPaG).

As this question carries the most marks on the exam paper, you should spend the most amount of time on this answer: 20 minutes. You may decide to complete this question first to avoid running out of time if left until the end.

This question will always contain a statement that gives an opinion on which factor was the most important reason for something happening. You should aim to write one paragraph on the factor stated in the question and at least one other paragraph on another factor. You should then write a concluding paragraph that sums up your argument on which factor was the most important reason.

You will be marked according to the following Assessment Objectives:

- AO1: demonstrate knowledge and understanding of the key features and characteristics of the period studied.

- AO2: explain and analyse historical events and periods studied using second-order historical concepts.

According to the mark scheme:

- Answers that don't get any marks will fail to answer the question.

- Level 1 answers (1–4 marks) will give a basic explanation of one or more factors.

- Level 2 answers (5–8 marks) will give a simple explanation of the stated factor **or** other factor(s), giving limited judgement.

- Level 3 answers (9–12 marks) will give a developed explanation of the stated factor **and** other factor(s), giving judgement.

- Level 4 answers (13–16 marks) will give a complex explanation of the stated factor and other factor(s), showing how they link and leading to a sustained judgement.

The best answers will:

- explain and analyse at least **TWO** causes of events and show how these factors link together

- show historical knowledge and understanding by including relevant details to support their analysis

- be well structured, and construct and develop an argument that is maintained throughout the answer, before reaching a conclusion.

Spelling, punctuation and grammar

You should always be careful to use correct spelling, punctuation and grammar in the exam. However, this is the question where you will actually be given up to 4 marks for the quality of your writing.

- Answers will receive a low mark (0–1) if there are spelling, punctuation and grammar mistakes that make the answer difficult to understand.

- Answers will receive 2 marks if the communication is fairly basic, with few key historical terms used.

- Answers will receive 3 or 4 marks if the quality of the historical communication is good and includes a range of key terms. This will help the examiner assess the historical knowledge and understanding, as the writing enhances the answer. It would be unusual for an answer that is less than a paragraph long to receive 3 or 4 marks.

It is therefore possible for students to communicate well and gain high marks for SPaG even though the answer is of low/no historical merit. So, you can boost your mark, to some extent, by the quality of your written response.

Here are some top tips for getting a good SPaG mark:

- Make sure you use capital letters at the start of sentences and for names of people and places.

- When you are revising, take time to learn the correct spelling of any difficult words. People's names are commonly misspelt, so pay attention to these.

- Take the time to learn as many key terms in the glossary as possible – you will get higher marks if you use specific vocabulary wherever you can.

- Do not use slang or informal language.

- Write in full sentences and use clear paragraphs, never bullet points.

The table below contains some key terms for this topic.

NAILIT!

Choose five of the more complicated words from the Glossary and write them out ten times (or until you can spell them correctly without looking). Try this again tomorrow and the next day until you can spell a range of subject specific words in time for the exam.

ideology	Cominform	Warsaw Pact	ICBM	space race
Cuban Missile Crisis	Vietcong	Détente	SALT 1	Truman Doctrine

DOIT!

1 Add or remove capitals where appropriate in the following: 'in berlin, the Wall was built almost Overnight'; Khrushchev; truman; Warsaw pact; 'Democratic freedoms were demanded'.

2 Make flash cards using the key terms in the table above. Add definitions on the back. Test yourself.

Answering the question

Below are four key events that this question may focus on followed by a table of causal factors (reasons).

1 Outbreak of the Cold War

2 Development of the Cold War 1945–49

3 Increasing tension in the 1950s

4 Increasing tension in the 1960s

a) Iron Curtain	e) Rigged elections	i) Berlin blockade
b) Truman Doctrine	f) Marshall Plan	j) Disagreements at Potsdam
c) Spread of communism	g) USA drops atom bombs on Japan	k) Contrasting attitudes and ideologies
d) The Berlin Wall	h) Bay of Pigs	l) Cuban Missile Crisis

DO IT!

1 Identify two causes in the table above that relate to each of the key topics above.

2 Identify a third cause (possibly not shown above) for each key event.

3 Explain how each factor identified helped to cause the event to happen.

4 Decide which of the three factors is the **main** or **most important** reason why the event happened. Explain why.

Linking causes

For higher level answers, it is important to show how causes link with each other.

For example, it could be argued that the failure to agree exactly what was meant by a 'Soviet sphere of influence' at the Potsdam Conference meant that Stalin felt he was justified in creating satellite states in Eastern Europe. However, the way in which the Soviets took control in those countries, i.e. rigged elections, meant that the spread of communism became a source of tension with the democratic West, as they feared for the stability of the free world.

DO IT!

1 Identify two or three causes from the table above that you think worked together to cause one of the events to happen.

2 Write a paragraph to explain how they link and caused the event.

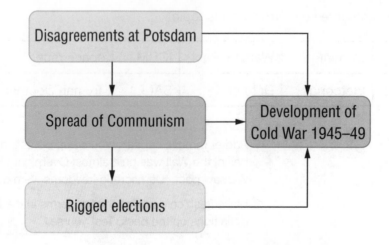

NAILIT!

Lists are a good way of managing and remembering information. Identify as many key events as you can from this topic and draw up a list of 3–5 causes for each event. This will be good preparation for the causation questions. You could refer to the timeline at the front of this book and then see how many you can write down from memory without turning back to have another look. Repeat this another day until you can remember more events each time.

Look at the exam-style question below.

AQA exam-style question

'The main reason for the development of the Cold War 1945–49 was the actions of the USA.'

How far do you agree with this statement?

Explain your answer.

(16 marks + 4 SPaG)

Step 1

Write a paragraph explaining how the reason given in the statement was important in causing the event.

In this case, the reason is the 'actions of the USA'. Therefore you need to write a paragraph explaining what some of these actions were and how they caused the development of the Cold War. You should directly answer the question in your first line by saying whether you agree, partly agree or disagree that the factor in the question was the most important reason.

For the main paragraphs of your essay, it is a good tip to use PEEL paragraphs:

- **Point** – This first sentence of the paragraph is the 'big point' that this paragraph will be about. In this case it will be that the actions of the USA were an important reason for the development of the Cold War.

- **Evidence** – You should follow the opening sentence with some specific evidence – facts, figures, names of people or places or events that help to prove your 'big point'. Use phrases such as 'a reason for this was ...', 'this was because ...'

- **Explain** – Then you should explain how the evidence you have provided actually does answer the question set. Key phrases to help link your answer back to the question are: 'therefore', 'this meant that', 'this led to'.

- **Link** – The top level answers will show how two or more reasons worked together to cause an event. Aim to include a sentence or two at the end of your paragraph providing a link to the reason you will write about in the next paragraph.

DOIT!

1 Take three highlighters and colour code the boxes in the table on page 68 to show which are the actions of the USA, which are the actions of the USSR, and which show shared responsibility for actions. You can leave blank if you feel the text box does not reveal actions of either country. Don't forget to include a key to show what the colours represent.

2 Decide on your opinion – who was most to blame or were they equally to blame?

3 Write a PEEL paragraph on how the actions of the USA caused the development of the Cold War. Remember that your first sentence should directly answer the question by saying whether you agree, partly agree or disagree.

DO IT!

Write a PEEL paragraph to show how the actions of the USSR caused the development of the Cold War.

DO IT!

Write a concluding paragraph to this essay that explains your opinion of whose actions were more to blame for developing the Cold War between 1945 and 1949.

NAIL IT!

You can achieve over half the marks for this question by writing two strong paragraphs on two factors, as long as one paragraph explains the factor given in the question itself.

Step 2

Write a paragraph explaining how another reason was important in causing the event.

In some cases there will be just one other reason possible. In the case of the question on page 69, this will be the actions of the USSR. As with your first paragraph you should explain what some of these actions were and how they caused the development of the Cold War.

Step 3

Write a third paragraph on another reason.

If you have time and there is another reason then write about it. If there are only two reasons then you could write another paragraph that supports your view on why one reason was most important or how factors worked together.

Step 4

Write a concluding paragraph giving a judgement that answers the question.

Notice the wording of the question: '**How far** do you agree with this statement?' You must explain if you:

- **agree** that the reason given in the statement is the most important by comparing that reason with another factor/s
- **partly agree** with the statement but show that there are other important **contributory factors** that worked together by comparing these reasons
- **disagree** with the statement and demonstrate that another factor is the most important reason by comparing it with the stated factor.

AQA exam-style question

'The main reason for the outbreak of the Cold War was **the contrasting attitudes and ideologies of the USA and USSR.**'

How far do you agree with this statement?

Explain your answer.

(16 marks + 4 SPaG)

Each paragraph begins by making a POINT – a reason for the outbreak of the Cold War. The first paragraph discusses the reason which is in the question statement.

The contrasting attitudes and ideologies of the USA and USSR were partly responsible for the outbreak of the Cold War. For example, the USA was a capitalist country whereas the USSR was a communist country. This meant that in the USA, the government was democratic and people enjoyed freedom of speech and on the whole fairly good living standards. However, in the USSR the government was a dictatorship and the people endured a below average standard of living. Both countries believed their ideology was the best and therefore these very different attitudes meant that some kind of conflict might occur because each country wanted to spread their ideology at the expense of the other's.

Tension between the two countries occurred following the end of the Second World War. For example, the USA and USSR were no longer fighting a common enemy - Nazi Germany - to keep them united. Following the defeat of Germany in April 1945, the USA secretly tested the first atom bomb; the USSR knew about the bomb and became suspicious of the USA, especially as there was now less reason for the two nations to stick together now that the war was at an end. This contributed to the outbreak of the Cold War.

Another factor that played a big part in the outbreak of the Cold War was Soviet expansion in Eastern Europe. By July 1945 Stalin's Red Army already controlled Poland, Czechoslovakia, Hungary, Romania, Bulgaria and the eastern part of Germany, and there was little the Allies could do about it. Stalin demanded a buffer zone to prevent further invasion of his country. It was agreed he could have a 'sphere of influence' and that there should be free elections, but many of the elections were fixed so that the Communists definitely won. This caused tensions and contributed to the outbreak of the Cold War because the West believed that this was part of Stalin's plan to dominate the whole of Europe.

In conclusion, the contrasting ideologies and attitudes of the USA and the USSR made tensions between the two superpowers possible, but their ideas had been different for many years and no conflict had occurred, so this is not the most important reason. It was only the events that followed the end of the war which made the contrasting ideologies seem more threatening and contributed to the outbreak of the Cold War. If the USA had not been secretive about the atom bomb or the USSR had not taken control of satellite states in Eastern Europe through fixed elections, the Cold War may never have happened.

> EVIDENCE is given to support each point. Some good knowledge and understanding is shown.

> The student EXPLAINS how each point was a reason for the outbreak of the Cold War.

> A concluding paragraph giving the student's judgement and reasons for this is given.

> LINKS between points are made, to show how together they contributed to the outbreak of the Cold War.

Sample answer

Read this student's answer to the question above. Ideally, answers will make links between factors at the end of each paragraph. Here is an example sentence that could appear at the end of paragraph 1 of the student's answer above, to show a link to the second reason explained in paragraph 2.

> This conflict occurred as a result of the USA and USSR feeling threatened by each other when the war came to an end, and this feeling of being threatened was made worse by the USA keeping the atom bomb secret.

DO IT!

1 Read the mark scheme information on page 66. What level do you think this student's answer would achieve?

2 Write a sentence to go at the end of the second paragraph that explains the link to the reason explained in the third paragraph.

Practice papers

Practice paper 1

Answer **all four** questions.

For this section, you will need to use the sources on page 74.

1 Study **Source A.**

Source A supports Truman's actions in Korea. How do you know?

Explain your answer using **Source A** and your contextual knowledge.

(4 marks)

2 Study **Sources B** and **C.**

How useful are **Sources B** and **C** to a historian studying opinions of the Marshall Plan?

Explain your answer using **Sources B** and **C** and your contextual knowledge.

(12 marks)

3 Write an account of how events in Czechoslovakia in 1968 increased Cold War tensions.

(8 marks)

4 'The main reason for the tension between the superpowers in the 1950s was the USSR's development of the atom bomb in 1949.'

How far do you agree with this statement?

Explain your answer.

(16 marks)
(SPaG 4 marks)

Practice paper 2

Answer **all four** questions.

For this section, you will need to use the sources on page 75.

1 Study **Source A.**

Source A criticises the actions of the USSR in Czechoslovakia.
How do you know?
Explain your answer using **Source A** and your contextual knowledge.

(4 marks)

2 Study **Sources B** and **C.**

How useful are **Sources B** and **C** to a historian studying the space race?

Explain your answer using **Sources B** and **C** and your contextual knowledge.

(12 marks)

3 Write an account of how the Potsdam Conference increased Cold War tensions.

(8 marks)

4 'The main reason for the tension between the superpowers in the 1950s was the Hungarian Uprising.'

How far do you agree with this statement?
Explain your answer.

(16 marks)
(SPaG 4 marks)

Sources for use with Practice paper 1

HISTORY DOESN'T REPEAT ITSELF

Source A This cartoon, by a British artist, is from 30 June 1950. It appeared in a British paper, *The Daily Herald*. Truman is leading the United Nations towards Korea. It reminds people of the failure of the League of Nations in the 1930s (the headstone says 'In Memory of the League of Nations. Died of Lack of Exercise Facing Wanton Aggression').

Source B A cartoon by E.H. Shepard published in the British *Punch* magazine on 18 June 1947. It shows Truman and Stalin as two bus drivers trying to get customers aboard. The 'customers' shown are Turkey, Hungary, Bulgaria, Austria.

THE RIVAL BUSES

Source C Andrei Vyshinsky, Soviet Representative on the United Nations Security Council, in a speech to the UN on the Truman Doctrine and the Marshall Plan, 18 September 1947.

It is becoming more and more evident to everyone that the implementation of the Marshall Plan will mean placing European countries under the economic and political control of the United States and direct interference by the latter in the internal affairs of those countries.

Moreover, this plan is an attempt to split Europe into two camps and, with the help of the United Kingdom and France, to complete the formation of a bloc of several European countries hostile to the interests of the democratic countries of Eastern Europe and most particularly to the interests of the Soviet Union.

Sources for use with Practice paper 2

"Of course, Mr. Dubcek, we've had to bring a few lady stenographers, one or two secretaries and some tea boys . . ."

Source A A cartoon by British artist Cummings, which appeared in a British newspaper in July 1968. Dubček, left, is holding a suitcase. Facing him are Soviet leaders. Brezhnev is in the middle. A 'Samovar' is a large Russian tea urn.

Source B Walt Disney (left) and Wehrner von Braun (right) in a photo from 1955. It shows some of the props used in a Disney film called 'Man and the Moon'. Von Braun was a Nazi rocket scientist, who then worked for the US space programme and appeared on Disney programmes in 1955. He would go on to work on the Saturn V rocket that landed on the Moon in 1969.

Source C Nikita Khrushchev speaking in November 1957, after the successful launch of Sputnik I and Sputnik II in October 1957. The Soviets had managed to get into space first, using the unmanned Sputnik craft.

The Sputniks prove that socialism has won the competition between socialist and capitalist countries … that the economy, science, culture, and the creative genius of the people in all spheres of life develop better and faster under socialism.

Doing well in your exam

This revision guide is designed to help you with Section B of your **Paper 1: Understanding the Modern World** exam.

Section A is the **Period Study**, which is accompanied by an **Interpretations Booklet**.

Section B is the **Wider World Study**, which is accompanied by a **Sources Booklet**.

You will have an answer booklet for Sections A and B, an interpretations booklet for Section A and a sources booklet for Section B. Check that you have the correct booklets for the topics you studied.

Assessment objectives

Your answers will be marked according to a mark scheme based on four assessment objectives (AOs). AOs are set by Ofqual and are the same across all GCSE History specifications and all exam boards:

AO1	demonstrate knowledge and understanding of the key features and characteristics of the period studied.
AO2	explain and analyse historical events and periods studied using second-order historical concepts (cause and consequence).
AO3	analyse, evaluate and use sources (contemporary to the period) to make substantiated judgements, in the context of historical events studied.
AO4	analyse, evaluate and make substantiated judgements about interpretations (including how and why interpretations may differ) in the context of historical events studied.

Paper 1 Section B covered in this guide examines AO1, AO2, and AO3. There will also be marks awarded for SPaG (Spelling, Punctuation and Grammar).

You must revise <u>all of the content</u> from the specification, as the questions in your exam could be on *any* of the topics listed. This guide is modelled on the specification so make sure you cover **all** the topics in this book.

There are four different types of question to answer in Section B:

Question 1	You will be given a contemporary source (a source from the historical period you are studying). There will be a statement about whether the source supports or criticises a country, organisation or person. The question will ask you, 'How do you know?'
Best answers ...	will describe key parts of the source and then add contextual knowledge (your own knowledge) to explain whether the source supports or criticises the event.
(4 marks) 5 minutes	The answer carries 4 marks so you do not have to write much. You will have approximately 5 minutes to answer this question.

📋 **Question 2**	You will be presented with **two** contemporary sources and asked how useful they are to a historian studying a particular event or historical issue.
✎ Best answers ...	will refer to the provenance of each source and add some contextual knowledge to reach a conclusion about the source's utility. You could try using the following method to help you remember what to include: **PAST**

P	Purpose	Ask why the source was produced.
A	Audience	Who did the source address?
S	Situation	Consider the situation of the author.
T	Test	Test against your own knowledge (contextual knowledge).

You should aim to write a paragraph for each of the two sources. Then write a concluding paragraph that actually answers the question 'how useful are the sources for studying ...' You must consider the particular event or issue stated in the question. You are not simply answering 'are the sources useful – in a general sense', the question is more specific than that.

TIP: A good conclusion might use the expression 'When taken together, the sources are both useful because ...' You might explain how the sources give different perspectives of people living at the time.

(12 marks) 18 minutes	This question is worth 12 marks. You will have approximately 18 minutes to answer the question, including time to study the sources.
📋 **Question 3**	This question asks you to write an account of an event.
✎ Best answers ...	will explain the lead up to the event or the event itself in chronological order. They will also link it clearly to the consequence of the event, for example increased international tension, and explain why that happened using phrases such as 'this led to', 'this meant that', 'consequently' and 'as a result'. You should aim to write two paragraphs explaining two aspects of the event and how one led to another.
(8 marks) 12 minutes	This question is worth 8 marks. You will have approximately 12 minutes to answer this question.

NAIL IT!

If you successfully follow the suggested timings, you will have time to study the sources carefully, and highlight and annotate them with your ideas, before you start writing.

Question 4	This question asks you how far you agree whether a factor was the main reason for something.	
	This question focuses on causation, and one key cause will have been provided for you in the question itself. Make sure you write a PEEL paragraph on that straight away.	

P	Point	This first sentence of the paragraph is the 'big point' that this paragraph will be about. In this case it will be that the actions of the USA were an important reason for the development of the Cold War.
E	Evidence	You should follow the opening sentence with some specific evidence - facts, figures, names of people or places or events that help to prove your 'big point'. Use phrases such as 'a reason for this was ...', 'this was because ...'
E	Explain	Then you should explain how the evidence you have provided actually does answer the question set. Key phrases to help link your answer back to the question are: 'therefore', 'this meant that', 'this led to'.
L	Link	The top level answers will show how two or more reasons worked together to cause an event. Aim to include a sentence or two at the end of your paragraph providing a link to the reason you will write about in the next paragraph.

Then you should aim to write AT LEAST one more PEEL paragraph on another cause that you know about, ideally another paragraph explaining another cause or your point of view.

Best answers ...	will provide a conclusion that attempts to show how reasons link together, or compare the causes and argue how one cause is more important than another.
(16 marks + 4 SPaG marks) *20 minutes*	This question carries 16 marks and therefore you should write the most for this answer. There are 4 additional marks available for spelling, punctuation and grammar (SPaG), so take care with your writing and check your work.
	You should aim to spend approximately 20 minutes on this question. You might consider answering this question first on Section B, so you don't run out of time.

Find past papers and mark schemes, and specimen papers, on the AQA website at www.aqa.org.uk/pastpapers.

Glossary

brinkmanship To take an issue to the brink (cliff-edge) of conflict.

Congress The branch of US government responsible for passing laws.

containment The US policy of 'containing' communism by stopping it spreading.

de-Stalinisation Ending the harsh and repressive policies associated with Stalin.

diplomat An official whose job is to represent one country in another, and who usually works in an embassy.

doctrine A statement of ideas.

dollar imperialism A policy of controlling a foreign country by providing them with financial assistance.

Domino Theory The idea that, like dominoes, if one country falls to communism, its neighbours will also do so – taken from Eisenhower's speech.

guerrilla warfare Small units of non-uniformed fighters would hit and run, disappearing into the general population, rather than fight as an army on a battlefield.

ICBM A nuclear missile capable of travelling 5500km or more and hitting other continents.

ideologies Belief system, usually political, for example capitalism or communism.

left-wing A left-wing person or group supports the political aims of groups such as socialists or communists.

peaceful co-existence The idea that communism and capitalism can both exist without each having to challenge the other.

Prague Spring Series of reforms to the communist state of Czechoslovakia, introduced by Alexander Dubček in 1968.

press censorship Forbidding publication, in newspapers, of material that would appear to criticise the government.

pressure point An area in which tensions remain high and conflict is very likely to occur between the two sides (East and West in this case).

Red Army The army of the Soviet Union.

reparations Compensation paid by the losers of the war to the victors.

satellite states Countries that are under the control of another country.

Soviet Union Another term for the USSR.

subjugation The action of bringing someone or something under domination or control.

US Secretary of State A senior government official mostly concerned with foreign policy.

USSR Union of Soviet Socialist Republics is the formal title of the Soviet Union. It was formed in 1922 and was made up of countries in Eastern Europe and North Asia. It was sometimes called 'Russia', as that was the largest of the republics.

Vietcong Vietnamese guerrilla fighters, often supplied by the Ho Chi Minh Trail.

Viet Minh Communist supporters of Ho Chi Minh in Vietnam.

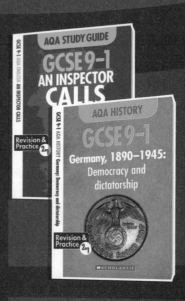